Gardening
Month by Month
in
Washington
and
Oregon

Aliso
Mariann

Lone Pine Publishing

© 2003 by Lone Pine Publishing
First printed in 2003   10 9 8 7 6 5 4 3 2 1
Printed in Canada

The Publisher: Lone Pine Publishing

10145 – 81 Avenue	1808 B Street NW, Suite 140
Edmonton, AB T6E 1W9	Auburn, WA
Canada	USA 98001

Website: www.lonepinepublishing.com

National Library of Canada Cataloguing in Publication Data

Beck, Alison, 1971–
   Gardening month by month in Washington and Oregon / Alison Beck and Marianne Binetti.

   ISBN 1-55105-359-4

   1. Gardening—Washington (State) 2. Gardening—Oregon. I. Binetti, Marianne, 1956– II. Title.
SB453.2.W3B42 2003   635'.09795   C2003-910120-7

Editorial Director: Nancy Foulds
Project Editor: Sandra Bit
Researchers: Don Williamson, Laura Peters, Carol Woo
Production Manager: Gene Longson
Design & Layout: Heather Markham
Maps & Climate Charts: Jeff Fedorkiw
Cover Design: Gerry Dotto
Principal Photographers: Tamara Eder, Tim Matheson, Robert Ritchie
Illustrations: Ian Sheldon
Scanning, Separations & Film: Elite Lithographers Co.

Front cover photographs (clockwise from top right): by Tamara Eder, false sunflower, poppy, sweet potato vine, climbing rose 'Lichtkonigen Lucia,' hybrid tea rose 'Just Joey'; *by Tim Matheson,* dahlia, daylily, cushion spurge.

The photographs in this book are reproduced with the generous permission of their copyright holders.

All other photos: All-American Selections 95c, 116–117, 123b, 129a; Therese D'Monte 66; Don Doucette 11a, 19a, 35c; Elliot Engley 27a, 27c, 29a, 29b; EuroAmerican 15a; Jennifer Fafard 119c, 121b, 121c, 123a, 125, 125c, 127a, 127b, 128–129, 137b, 147a, 147b, 147c, 151c; Anne Gordon 133b; Horticolor©Nova-Photographik/Horticolor 90; Colin Laroque 92–93; Dawn Loewen 39c; Erika Markham 113b; Heather Markham 53b, 71a, 75c; Kim O'Leary 3b, 25b, 107a, 143b; Alison Penko 6–7, 23c, 109c ; Laura Peters 77c, 77d, 111a, 115c; Peter Thompstone 41b, 47c, 101a, 141a; Don Williamson 115a, 131a, 140–141, 144.

Frost dates maps: information from the website of the National Oceanic and Atmospheric Administration, National Climatic Data Center, Asheville, North Carolina (www.ncdc.noaa.gov/climatedata.html);
Hardiness zones map: based on the USDA Plant Hardiness Zones Map; *Climate normals and extremes charts:* data adapted with permission from the Western Regional Climate Center website, http://www.wrcc.dri.edu/COMPARATIVE.html.

This book is not intended as a 'how-to' guide for eating garden plants. No plant or plant extract should be consumed unless you are certain of its identity and toxicity and of your potential for allergic reactions.

We acknowledge the financial support of the Government of Canada through the Book Publishing Industry Development Program (BPIDP) for our publishing activities.

PC: 08

There is no single way to describe gardening in the Pacific Northwest. The climate, soil conditions, day length, season length and altitude vary greatly from area to area, creating a unique experience in every garden and for every gardener. Spring can arrive anytime between February and June in the different areas of this region. Here we find one of the mildest climates in the United States as well as one of the harshest.

The two main influences are the ocean and the mountains. Along the Coast, warm moist air travels in from the Pacific and rises when it reaches the mountains, creating a moderate climate with a distinctively wet season along Coastal areas. The mountains also prevent a lot of moisture from traveling farther Inland, giving Inland gardeners a much drier climate.

The summers tend to be cool to warm on the Coast and hotter Inland. Rain is plentiful in fall, winter and spring along the Coast with a dry period in summer continuing into fall. Inland rainfall can be quite scarce during the growing season, but snowfall is reliable for many Inland and mountain gardens.

Caryopteris with ornamental grasses

The soil along the Coast tends to be acidic while soil Inland tends to be alkaline.

Though there are vast differences between Coastal gardens and Inland gardens, many of the same plants thrive in both locations. Many plants are capable of adapting to a wide variety of conditions, and though some of the tender, exotic plants are hardy only in sheltered gardens near the Coast, a wealth of beautiful plants can be enjoyed by all of this region's gardeners.

climbing rose 'Lichtkonigen Lucia'

Every imaginable style of garden can be and probably has been created here, from free-form English-style cottage gardens to cool, moist woodland gardens and from Zen-like Japanese gardens to formal knot gardens. These gardens reflect the style and enthusiasm of the gardeners and the diversity of situations in which they garden.

Where we garden varies almost as much as what we garden. Apartment and condo dwellers enjoy container gardening; rural gardeners may be tilling the same soil that generations of their ancestors did; urban gardens include those in older neighborhoods with deeper topsoil and those whose new gardens may have only the thin layer of soil the construction company returned to their yards. Beautiful, successful gardens are possible in every situation, limited only by the imagination of the gardener.

The climate poses different challenges for gardeners throughout the Pacific Northwest, so some research and experimentation are required to get the best results from your garden. Learning what to expect and when to expect it as well as what plants are best suited to your garden are key elements to gardening.

The Chase Garden, Orting, WA

Mid- to late summer and early fall are usually dry for the entire region, with moist or downright wet weather the rest of the year along the Coast and dry or cold weather the remainder of the year Inland. Inconsistent rainfall during all or part of the growing season can be overcome through the use of drought-resistant plants and increasing the water-holding potential of your soil by adding compost and by mulching. Locally native plants can be good choices for gardeners, too, because these are plants that are accustomed to the peculiarities of the local soil and climate and are able to thrive in them.

During the growing season, adequate precipitation can make the difference between gardening success or failure. In a good year, regular rainfall takes care of all our watering

gazanias

bridge pathway (*above*); mini alpine garden (*below*)

naturalistic water feature (*below*)

needs and only hanging baskets and beds beneath the overhang of the house need to be watered. In a bad year, it seems as if it will never stop raining or that it will never rain again. Although rainfall is fairly dependable, droughts and deluges are always possible. As with all the factors that influence our gardens, we must be prepared to make the most of what nature offers us and try to take up the slack where it lets off.

The length of the growing season also varies greatly. Some Inland and higher altitude gardeners may have barely 90 frost-free days to work with, while some of their Coastal counterparts enjoy 280 days between the last and first frost dates. A lack of heat and dry weather even when there is no frost can delay some plants from maturing, even along the Coast. So plant selection is important in every garden, despite any perceived advantages or disadvantages.

Many of the gardening books available to us are written by and for gardeners in climates very different from our own. Most of the general information about gardening is accurate and useful, but we must learn through experimentation what works best in our own gardens.

The purpose of this book is to give you ideas and to help you plan what should be done and when. Garden tasks are listed in the month they should be completed, and general ideas that can be applied in a variety of months are also included. Garden tasks are divided loosely for Coastal and Inland gardeners as some tasks will need to be completed at different times for gardeners in these two general areas. Pay attention to your own climate and garden to decide the best time to complete the suggested task. Plenty of space is also included for you to write in your own thoughts and ideas. Keep the book handy, and jot information down year in and year out, all year round.

The information in this book is general. If you need more detailed information on a topic, refer to the resources listed at the back of the book. Your local library is also an

a xeriscape planting

excellent place to search for the information you need. Gardening courses are offered through colleges, continuing education programs, gardening societies and through Master Gardener programs. You can tackle even the most daunting garden task once you are prepared and well informed.

Use this book to keep track of unusual weather conditions, when plants sprout and when they first flower. Make note of the birds and insects you see in the garden. If a plant gave you a lot of trouble in a certain location, you will remember not to put it in the same location next year if you

golden marguerite

add that comment to your book. Jot down your fantastic inspirations for future gardening design plans. If you see an unfamiliar and exciting plant at a garden center or in a neighborhood garden, you can make a note to look it up later. Write down anything about your garden that tickles your fancy. You'll appreciate it next spring when memories of this year's garden are getting a little fuzzy.

There are no absolute rules when it comes to gardening. No two years are identical, and all information should be taken with a pinch of salt. Use your own best judgment when deciding when to do things in your garden. If spring has been cold and wet you may have to plant later than suggested, or earlier if an early spring warms things up quickly.

Above all else, always take time to enjoy your Pacific Northwest garden.

mixed border (*above*)
hot peppers (*below*)

JANUARY

*Now is the time to plan and
dream of the summer and the
garden yet to be.*

JANUARY

1

2

Avoid using chemical de-icers because they are harmful to lawns and garden plants.

3

4

If you had a real Christmas tree, cut it up and use the branches as a mulch to shelter low-growing shrubs and groundcovers instead of recycling it.

5

6

7

One of the flowers you might dream of adding to your garden in spring is the beautiful hybrid tea 'Loving Memory' (left). This rose will flourish in most gardens.

Cotoneaster (*right*)

Interior/Inland gardens are likely to be blanketed by snow while **Coastal gardens** are in the midst of the rainy season. Plants that dislike waterlogged conditions may rot in Coastal gardens, and tender plants may suffer in the Interior/Inland if they are not covered by a sufficient amount of snow. South-facing walls are warmer than other areas of the garden, and flowerbeds under the eaves of the house are likely to stay driest. Pay attention to these special growing conditions, and you'll be able to use them to your advantage when designing and maintaining your garden.

THINGS TO DO

Rain, frost, snow—no matter where we garden, we can expect our chilliest weather in January.

ALL GARDENS

Clean the foliage of your houseplants. When light levels are low, it is important for plants to be able to use whatever light is available. As a bonus, you might help reduce insect populations because their eggs will likely be wiped off along with the dust.

Don't forget to top up your bird-feeders regularly. Feeding the birds encourages them to keep visiting in summer when they will help keep your insect pest populations under control.

Order gardening and seed catalogues to look through even if you don't start your own seeds. Order early for the best selection. Choose and order seeds for early starting. Sort through the seeds you have, test them for viability (see p. 13) and throw out any that don't germinate or that you won't grow. Trade seeds with gardening friends.

JANUARY

8

9

Avoid placing houseplants in hot or cold drafts.

10

11

Reduce watering of houseplants because most need little water during winter.

12

13

14

Begonias (*left*) can be brought indoors in fall and kept as houseplants in a sunny location through the winter.

Gently brush snow off the branches of evergreens such as cedars, but leave any ice that forms to melt naturally. The weight of the snow or ice can permanently bend flexible branches, but more damage is done trying to remove ice than is done through its weight.

COAST

Cut the branches of spring-flowering shrubs for forcing indoors.

Many summer- and fall-flowering trees, shrubs and perennials can be pruned this month, but don't prune plants that flower on old wood.

Start perennial seeds indoors for spring planting. Seed-starting tips are listed in February (p. 29).

Dormant trees, shrubs, vines and perennials can be planted out but avoid working with the soil when it is very wet because you can damage the structure.

Containers with tender plants such as rosemary should be moved to a sheltered location when cold weather or snow is expected.

Annual poppy seeds are easy to collect and share with friends. There are many color choices available in both single- (*Iceland poppies, center right*) and double-flowering (*peony-flowered poppies, top right and below*) varieties.

To test older seeds for viability, place 10 seeds between two layers of moist paper towel and put them in a sealed container. Keep the paper evenly dampened but not too wet. Seeds may rot if the paper towel is too moist. Check each day to see if the seeds have sprouted. If less than half the seeds sprout, buy new ones.

JANUARY

15

16

Check houseplants regularly for common indoor insect pests such as whiteflies, spider mites and mealybugs.

17

18

19

20

An English ivy topiary (*left*) makes a nice addition to a spring planter.

Coleus (*top right*); ficus (*bottom right*)

INTERIOR/INLAND

Snow is the garden's best friend. Pile clean snow on snowless garden beds to insulate them against the wind and cold. Some people refer to this as 'snow farming.'

Water shrubs and evergreens during winter thaws if there is no snow around them. Water the ground around the plants, but don't worry if some water freezes onto the branches—the ice won't hurt them.

If the snow cover is inconsistent, keep mulches topped up to protect plants from temperature fluctuations and to reduce water loss.

GARDEN DESIGN

January is a great time for garden planning. In winter, the bones of the garden are laid bare, so you can take a good look at the garden's overall structure.

Imagine the garden you'd like to have, and keep a notebook and your diagrams handy so you can jot down ideas as they come to you.

As you look out your windows at the winter landscape, think about what could make your garden look more attractive in winter. Features such as birdbaths, ponds, benches, decks and winding pathways improve the look and function of your garden year-round. Persistent fruit, unusual bark and branch patterns, evergreens and colorfully stemmed shrubs also provide winter interest.

Most indoor plants will benefit from increased humidity levels. Place pots on a tray of pebbles. If you add water to the pebbles when needed, you will increase the humidity through evaporation but prevent water-logged roots.

JANUARY

21

22

Get lawn mowers and other power tools serviced now. They will be ready for use in spring, and you may get a better price before the spring rush.

23

24

Interior/Inland gardeners *may want to bring over-wintering geraniums out from storage within the next few weeks.*

25

26

27

These trees and shrubs will add interest to your garden in winter: kerria (*left*), autumn flowering cherry and viburnum (*top right*), amur maple (*center right*) and Japanese maple.

Plants that add variety to a winter garden:

- Cedar (*Thuja*), False Cypress (*Chamaecyparis*) or Juniper (*Juniperus*): evergreen branches
- Clematis (*Clematis*): fuzzy seed-heads
- Corkscrew Hazel (*Corylus*): twisted and contorted branches
- Cotoneaster (*Cotoneaster*): persistent red berries
- Dogwoods (*Cornus*): red, purple or yellow stems
- Highbush Cranberry (*Viburnum trilobum*): bright red berries
- Kerria (*Kerria*): bright green stems
- Maples (*Acer ginnala*, *Acer palmatum*): attractive bark and branching patterns
- Shrub Roses (*Rosa*): brightly colored hips
- Winged Euonymus (*Euonymus alatus*): corky ridges on the branches
- Autumn Flowering Cherry (*Prunus subhirtella autumnalis*): very early flowering

JANUARY

28

29

In a mild winter, **Coastal gardeners** *may see hardy perennials (e.g., snapdragons) and flowering cherry trees blooming this month.*

30

31

Woody evergreens, such as cedar (*left*), upright juniper (*top right*) and white spruce (*far right*), add interesting texture and rich green color to a sometimes monotonous winter landscape.

PROBLEM AREAS IN THE GARDEN

Keep track of these potential problem areas in your garden.

- windswept areas: perhaps a tree, shrub or hedge could be added next summer to provide shelter
- snowfree areas: places where snow is always quick to melt are poor choices for very tender plants, which benefit most from the protection of the snow
- snowbound areas: places where snow is slowest to melt provide the most protection to plants but stay frozen longest in spring, making them poor locations for spring-flowering plants
- waterlogged areas: places where water is slow to drain or even pools during extended wet periods are poor locations for plants that need well-drained soil
- dry areas: places that rarely get wet and drain quickly when they do shouldn't be used for plants that need a lot of moisture
- erosion-prone areas: rain can quickly wash the soil away from slopes, so consider planting groundcovers to hold the soil to the slope.

Spruce are widely grown and new varieties are available almost every gardening season. They are well suited to cold winters, and some, such as the Colorado blue spruce (left), provide wonderful winter color against brilliant white snow.

FEBRUARY

The longer days and spells of warm weather turn our thoughts to the upcoming gardening season.

FEBRUARY

1

2

*Finish ordering plants
and seeds from catalogs.*

3

4

*Check shrubs and trees for storm-damaged
branches, and remove them using proper
pruning techniques.*

5

6

7

Colorful little crabapples often remain on the
branches of the tree through winter, a reminder of
the beautiful blossoms to come in spring
(*left and top right*). Maple with early
spring flowers, flowering crabapple
trees in spring (*bottom right*)

Groundhog Day is a reminder that the worst of winter is over and that spring will soon be here. The rain or snow may continue to fall freely on the Coast, but a few dry days may find **Coastal gardeners** out digging the garden. **Interior/Inland gardeners** may start seeds indoors and should keep a close eye on the garden during warm, potentially dry spells, when watering may be needed.

THINGS TO DO

February is a great month for making preparations that will keep things moving smoothly once the season kicks into high gear.

ALL GARDENS

As the days start to lengthen, indoor plants may start to show signs of new growth. Increase watering and apply a weak fertilizer ($1/4$ strength) only after they begin to grow.

Interior/Inland gardeners can cut branches of flowering shrubs, such as forsythia, crabapple and cherry, to bring indoors. Placed in a bright location in a vase of water, they will begin to flower, providing a taste of spring in winter.

FEBRUARY

8

9

Continue to check for insect pests on your houseplants.

10

11

Coastal gardeners *can start preparing garden beds for spring planting.*

12

13

14

Dianthus (*left*), browallia (*top right*), bellflower (*far right*) and begonia (*near right*) are plants you can start from seed in February.

Start seeds for annuals, perennials and vegetables that are slow to mature. A few to consider are

- Amethyst Flower (*Browallia*)
- Begonia (*Begonia*)
- Bellflower (*Campanula*)
- Geranium (*Pelargonium*)
- Hollyhock (*Alcea*)
- Lady's Mantle (*Alchemilla*)
- Peppers (*Capsicum*)
- Pinks (*Dianthus*)
- Tomatoes (*Lycopersicon*)

Apply all-season horticultural oil (also called dormant oil), used to control overwintering insects, to trees, shrubs and vines before the buds swell. Follow the directions carefully to avoid harming beneficial insects. Avoid using horticultural oil on blue-needled evergreens, such as blue spruce. This treatment takes the blue off the existing needles, though the new needles will be blue.

FEBRUARY

15

16

Coastal gardeners can cut back and tidy up last year's perennial growth. Avoid damaging any new shoots that might be emerging.

17

18

Check to see if any of the tubers or bulbs you are storing indoors have started to sprout. Pot them and keep them in a bright location once they do.

19

20

21

Many varieties of dahlia (*left*) can be started from seed in February for transplanting after the danger of frost has passed.

Fresh herbs growing in a greenhouse in winter (*center right*); seed tray, pots, soil and spray mister for indoor seeding (*bottom right*)

COAST

In our rainy climate, salts can leach quickly from the soil, leaving it too acidic for some plants, including lawns. A dusting in spring and fall with dolomitic lime can help balance the pH of your lawn's soil. Follow package directions, and use a spreader to apply the correct amount. A soil test will tell you what quantities are needed.

❦

Slugs are a problem in spring and fall. Avoid watering at night when slugs are most active. Handpicking them off plants or from their hiding places (under boards, debris) is the best way to eliminate them. A compost pile can be a source of slugs, so keep compost away from your most tender plants.

❦

Plants that tolerate or enjoy cooler weather, such as pansies, primroses and snapdragons, can be planted now. Seeds for plants such as poppies, peas, bachelor's buttons, spinach and pot marigolds can be direct-sown now. Be prepared to cover young seedlings during exceptionally cold weather.

INTERIOR/INLAND

During dry, warm spells, water plants not covered by snow.

Seedlings will be weak and floppy if they don't get enough light. Consider purchasing a fluorescent or other grow light (above) to provide extra illumination for them.

22

23

*Dormant bare-root plants can be planted
out now in **Coastal gardens**.*

24

25

*Although many seeds do not require
light to germinate, the seeds of heat-loving
plants (peppers, tomatoes) need warmth to
sprout. Keep these seeds at about
75°F (24°C) to aid germination.*

26

27

28

29

The floribunda rose 'Fellowship/Livin' Easy' (*left*)
is well known for its reliable vigor, attractive foliage
and showy, long-lived blooms. It also makes a great
cut flower.

STARTING SEEDS

What you will need for starting seeds:

- containers to grow them in, such as pots, trays or peat pots
- sterile soil mix intended for starting seeds
- plastic bags or tray covers to keep the seedbed humid
- a hand-held spray mister for watering and a heating coil or pad to keep seeds evenly heated (optional).

Tips for starting seeds:

- Moisten the soil before you fill the containers.

- Firm the soil down in the containers, but don't pack it too tightly.

- Leave seeds that require light for germination uncovered.

- Plant large seeds individually by poking a hole in the soil with the tip of a pen or pencil and then dropping the seed in the hole.

- Spread small seeds evenly across the soil surface, then lightly cover with more soil mix.

- To spread small seeds, place them in the crease of a folded piece of paper and gently tap the bottom of the fold to roll them onto the soil.

- Mix very tiny seeds, like those of begonia, with very fine sand before planting to spread them out more evenly.

- Plant only one type of seed in each container. Some seeds will germinate before others, and it is difficult to keep both seeds and seedlings happy in the same container.

- Cover pots or trays of seeds with clear plastic to keep them moist.

- Seeds do not need bright, direct light to germinate and can be kept in an out-of-the-way place until they begin to sprout.

To prevent seedlings from damping-off, always use a sterile soil mix, thoroughly clean containers before using them, maintain good air circulation around seedlings and water from the bottom to keep the soil moist, not soggy.

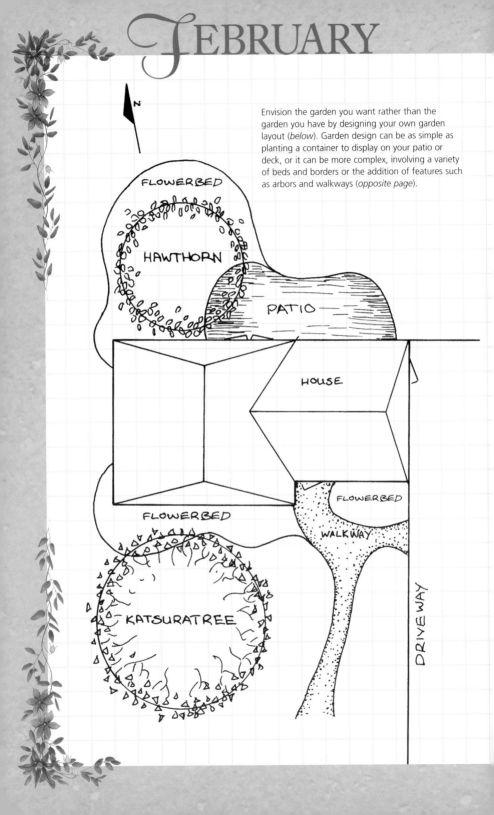

Envision the garden you want rather than the garden you have by designing your own garden layout (*below*). Garden design can be as simple as planting a container to display on your patio or deck, or it can be more complex, involving a variety of beds and borders or the addition of features such as arbors and walkways (*opposite page*).

N

FLOWERBED

HAWTHORN

PATIO

HOUSE

FLOWERBED

FLOWERBED

WALKWAY

KATSURA TREE

DRIVE WAY

Tips for growing healthy seedlings:

- To prevent crowding, transplant seedlings to individual containers once they have three or four true leaves.

- Space plants so that the leaves do not overshadow those of neighboring plants.

- Keep seedlings in the brightest location available to reduce stretching.

- Don't fertilize young seedlings. Wait until the seed leaves (the first leaves to appear) have begun to shrivel, then fertilize with a weak fertilizer once a week.

- Once the seeds germinate, keep the seedlings in a bright location and remove the plastic cover.

MARCH

Spring is in full swing on the Coast while Interior/Inland gardeners are just seeing the first signs that winter is coming to an end.

MARCH

1

2

Start or continue indoor seeding. Most vegetable and flowers seeds only need to be started a few weeks before they are planted out.

3

4

Water houseplants that start sprouting new growth more frequently, and apply a weak fertilizer.

5

6

When designing your garden, consider planting a fast-growing, drought-tolerant elder (*left and near right*). The elder's showy foliage adds color and texture to a landscape, and its edible berries can be made into jelly or wine or left for the birds.

Red-twigged dogwoods (*far right*) can be pruned now, but flowering dogwoods (*top right*) should be pruned after flowering.

7

Warm spells lure us out to see what's sprouting and blooming, and early spring flowering plants herald the start of another gardening season. **Coastal gardens** are heading into full spring bloom while **Interior/Inland gardens** are just beginning to sprout. Late spring frosts are still likely in the Interior/Inland, so gardeners should be prepared to push mulch back over tender young shoots if a frost is expected.

THINGS TO DO

The desire to dig, prune and get our hands in the soil gets us out in the garden in March.

ALL GARDENS

Prune late-flowering shrubs (July or later) and shrubs grown for colorful young growth, for example, barberry.

MARCH

8

9

Coastal gardeners should check for pests that feed on new growth.

10

11

Interior/Inland gardeners can clear beds of debris and start digging once the ground has thawed and the soil is dry enough to work.

12

13

14

As soon as the snow begins to melt in spring, the leaves of the bergenia become visible and are quickly followed by its pretty magenta flowers (*left*).

Spirea (*top right*); hardy kiwi (*center right*); 'Annabelle' hydrangea (*bottom right*)

Before doing any digging, call your utility companies to locate any buried wires, cables or pipes to prevent injury and save time and money.

Keep off your lawn when it is frozen, bare of snow and/or very wet to avoid damaging the grass or compacting the soil.

Plants to prune in spring
- False Spirea (*Sorbaria sorbifolia*)
- Hardy Kiwi (*Actinidia arguta*)
- Hydrangea (*Hydrangea*), some varieties
- Japanese Spirea (*Spirea japonica*)
- Potentilla (*Potentilla*)
- Red-twig Dogwood (*Cornus alba*)
- Yellow or Purple-leafed Elders (*Sambucus*)

MARCH

15

16

On the Coast, *gardeners should begin to harden off the young plants that you plan to plant out next month.*

17

18

Interior/Inland gardeners *should cut back old perennial growth to make way for the new.*

19

20

21

Lilies are long-lived, easy-to-grow perennials. They look superb in floral arrangements combined with flowers such as baby's breath (*left*).

If planted early enough in spring, clematis (*top right*) flowers the first summer; forsythia in bloom (*far right*); basket-of-gold and tulips in a gorgeous spring-blooming bed (*bottom right*).

COAST

Apply compost to established beds and gently work it into the soil.

Stake plants that need peony hoops or twiggy supports now while they are young. They will fill in to cover the support over the summer.

If a plant needs well-drained soil and full sun to thrive, it will be healthiest and best able to fight off problems in those conditions. Work with your plants' natural tendencies.

MARCH

22

23

Clean and disinfect your birdhouses and feeders to remove old seeds and lessen the potential for disease.

24

25

Remove containers before planting. Plastic and fiber pots restrict root growth and prevent plants from becoming established.

26

27

28

Rhododendrons (*left*) grow well and look good when planted in groups. They thrive in sheltered locations and require fertile, acidic, moist and well-drained soil to do well.

Flowering quince (*top right*); goat's beard (*bottom right*)

INTERIOR/INLAND

As the snow melts, start clearing up the debris in your yard, such as leaves, sticks, garbage and doggie poop.

Days can be warm enough to encourage some plants to start sprouting. Pull mulch back to let in the light and air, but be prepared to re-cover plants if heavy frost is expected.

PLANTING TIPS

Early spring is prime planting season. Trees, shrubs, vines and perennials often establish most quickly when they are planted just as they are about to break dormancy. They are full of growth hormones, and they recover quickly from transplant shock.

A few things to keep in mind when planting your garden:

- Never work with your soil when it is very wet or very dry.
- Avoid planting during the hottest, sunniest part of the day. Choose an overcast day, or plant early or late in the day.
- Prepare your soil before you plant to avoid damaging roots later.
- Get your new plants into the ground as soon as possible when you get them home. Roots can get hot and dry out quickly in containers. Keep plants in a shady spot if you must wait to plant them.
- Most plants are happiest when planted at the same depth they have always grown at. Trees, in particular, can be killed by too deep a planting.
- Plants should be well watered when they are newly planted. Watering deeply and infrequently will encourage the strongest root growth.

Don't plant vigorous spreaders in rock gardens with tiny alpine plants or large shrubs right next to walkways.

MARCH

29

The single most important thing you can do when planting is to make sure you have the right plant in the right location. Consider the mature size of the plant and its cultural requirements.

30

31

The splendid yellow shrub rose 'Morden Sunrise' (*below*) is a hardy yellow rose that should grow well in most gardens.

● Check the root zone before watering. The soil surface may appear dry when the roots are still moist.

Harden annuals and perennials off before planting them by gradually exposing them to longer periods of time outside on a porch or deck. Doing so gives your plants time to adapt to outdoor weather conditions and reduces the chance of transplant shock.

Remove only damaged branches when planting trees or shrubs, and leave the plant to settle in for at least one year before you begin any formative pruning. Plants need all the branches and leaves they have when they are trying to get established.

Trees less than 1.5 m (5') tall, such as this young tree (*above*), do not need staking unless they are in a very windy location. Unstaked trees develop stronger root systems.

staking a tree properly

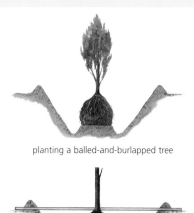

planting a balled-and-burlapped tree

planting a bare-root tree

APRIL

*Spring begins to arrive as
the month progresses, and more and more
gardeners enjoy frost-free days.*

APRIL

1

2

Check your power tools, such as the lawn mower, and have them serviced if you didn't do it over winter.

3

4

Coastal gardeners *can divide perennials that bloom in mid-summer or later, such as asters, daylilies and sedums.*

5

6

7

The columbine (*left*) is a beautiful flower that some say resembles a bird in flight. Its jewel-like colors herald the coming of summer.

Clockwise from top right: primroses; foxgloves; marigolds

We are most attracted to plants that are in full bloom. To avoid having a one-season garden, visit your garden center regularly over the spring, summer and fall. Plants that are flowering at different times will catch your eye and give you a chance to fill your garden with a diverse selection of plants.

The warm days of spring are welcome—**Coastal gardeners** anticipate the end of the rainy season and **Interior/Inland gardeners** see fewer and lighter frosts. We are eager to be in the garden to see what is sprouting or blooming. We finish our tidying, continue or begin our plantings and watch as our gardens awaken.

THINGS TO DO

The real gardening work is under-way—raking, digging, planting and pruning. We begin the hard work now that will let us sit back and enjoy the garden once summer arrives.

APRIL

8

9

Repot houseplants if needed.

10

11

Coastal gardeners *can begin to harden off houseplants that will be moved into the garden for the summer.*

12

13

14

Consider planting daylilies (*left and top right*) this spring. Though each bloom lasts only a day, these lilies are easygoing, prolific and versatile, and come in an almost infinite variety of forms, sizes and colors.

ALL GARDENS

If you can't plant them right away, store any plants you purchase in as bright a location as possible but out of direct sunlight. Harden them off by placing them outdoors for a short period each day.

Cool, wet spring weather can cause some drought-loving plants to rot. Improve soil drainage by adding organic matter.

COAST

Snapdragons, spiderflowers and tomatoes can be started from seed only a few weeks before moving them into the garden. Consider making several plantings of fewer plants at a time to prolong blooming periods and to ensure that all your fruits or vegetables aren't ripening at the same time.

Once the last frost date has passed in your region (p. 159) and the soil has warmed up, tender annuals and vegetable plants can be planted out. A floating row cover can help the soil warm up and offers young seedlings some protection from heavy rain.

Seeds sown directly into the garden may take longer to germinate than those planted indoors, but the resulting plants, such as Iceland poppies (below), will be stronger.

APRIL

15

16

Coastal gardeners should prune spring-flowering shrubs and trees once they are finished blooming.

17

18

Interior/Inland gardeners can plant trees, shrubs and vines once the soil can be worked.

19

20

21

A traditional garden favorite, sweet peas (*left*) are easy to grow from seed in early spring. They sprout quickly and have sweetly scented blooms that can be cut often for fragrant indoor bouquets.

Clockwise from top right: phlox, cabbage, rocket larkspur and nigella be planted before the last spring frost

Many plants prefer to grow in cool weather and can be started well before the last frost. These seeds can be direct sown as soon as the soil can be worked:

- Bachelor's Buttons (*Centaurea cyanus*)
- Cabbage (*Brassica oleracea*)
- Calendula (*Calendula officinalis*)
- California Poppy (*Eschscholzia californica*)
- Godetia (*Clarkia amoena*)
- Kale (*Brassica napus*)
- Love-in-a-Mist (*Nigella damascena*)
- Peas (*Pisum sativum*)
- Phlox (*Phlox drummondii*)
- Poppy (*Papaver rhoeas*)
- Rocket Larkspur (*Consolida ajacis*)
- Spinach (*Spinacea oleracea*)
- Sweet Pea (*Lathyrus odoratus*)
- Swiss Chard (*Beta vulgaris*)

22

23

Prune plants according to your style and taste.

24

25

Interior/Inland gardeners *should bring garden tools out of storage and examine them for rust or other damage. Clean and sharpen them if you didn't before you put them away in fall.*

26

27

28

You can depend on aubretia (*left*) to put on a great floral show in spring.

Clockwise from top right: spiral juniper; pompom cedar; formally pruned yew hedge and cedars

INTERIOR/INLAND

Take a trip to a garden center. The best selection of uncommon annuals and perennials is available early, and you may be able to purchase woody plants while they are still dormant. Many garden centers will take your name and call you when the plants you are looking for arrive.

Avoid working your soil until it has thawed and dried out a bit. A handful of thawed soil should squeeze into a ball that holds its shape but breaks apart easily when pressed with a thumb or finger.

PRUNING TIPS

Prune trees and shrubs to maintain the health and attractive shape of a plant, to increase the quality and yield of fruit, to control and direct growth and to create interesting plant forms and shapes.

Once you learn how to prune plants correctly, it is an enjoyable garden task. There are many good books available on the topic of pruning. One is listed at the back of this book. If you are unsure about pruning, take a pruning course, often offered by garden centers, botanical gardens and adult education programs.

Don't prune trees or shrubs when growth has started and buds are swelling. Prune before growth starts in spring or wait until plants have leafed out.

PRUNING TIPS

- Prune at the right time of year. Trees and shrubs that flower before June, usually on the previous year's wood, should be pruned after they have flowered. Trees and shrubs that flower after June, usually on new growth, can be pruned in spring.

- Use the correct tool for the size of branch to be removed: hand pruners (secateurs), for growth up to $^3/_4$" (2 cm) in diameter; long-handled loppers for growth up to $1^1/_2$" (4 cm) in diameter; or a pruning saw for growth up to about 6" (15 cm) in diameter.

- Always use clean, sharp tools.

- Always use hand pruners (secateurs) or loppers with the blade side towards the plant and the hook towards the part to be removed.

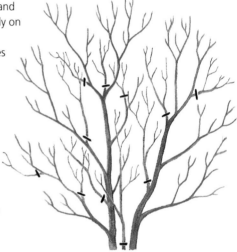

thinning cuts

Thin trees and shrubs to promote the growth of younger, healthier branches. Doing so rejuvenates a plant.

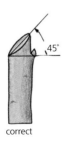

correct

too low

angle too great

too high

PROPER PRUNING CUTS

When pruning, avoid the following:

- Don't leave stubs. Whether you are cutting off a large branch or deadheading a lilac, always cut back to a join. Branches should be removed to the branch collar, and smaller growth should be cut back to a bud or branch union. There is no absolute set angle for pruning, but generally a 45° angle is preferable. Each plant should be pruned according to its individual needs.

- Never use pruning paint or paste. Trees have a natural ability to create a barrier between living and dead wood. Painting over a cut impairs this ability.

- Avoid cutting off the top of a tree, or 'topping.' Topping is not good for a tree's overall health. It also causes a tree to send out too many side shoots at the top. Excessive top growth destabilizes a tree and leads it to fall in high winds.

Never try to remove a tree or large branch by yourself. Have someone help you, or hire a professional to do it. Always hire an ISA (International Society of Arboriculture) certified professional to remove branches on trees growing near power lines or other hazardous areas, especially if they could damage a building, fence or car if they were to fall. Branches and trees are usually much heavier than anticipated and can do a lot of damage if they fall in the wrong place.

MAY

*Even in the coldest areas, gardeners can finally
celebrate the arrival of warm weather because
they know that summer will soon be here.*

MAY

1

2

Coastal gardeners should start new garden beds or expand and improve old ones.

3

4

Interior/Inland gardeners should remove mulch from perennials and trim back and clear away any of last year's growth if it was still too cold to do so in April.

5

6

7

The Japanese anemone or windflower (*left*) is an attractive plant at all stages. Some species bloom in spring while others reserve their lovely displays for fall.

Saucer magnolia (*top right*) flowers in mid- to late spring; lilacs (*bottom right*) do well in colder climates because they need freezing temperatures to set their flowers.

May weather can be unpredictable, one year warm and sunny and the next cold and wet. **Coastal gardeners** finally enjoy some drier weather and the display of late-spring and early-summer bloomers such as lilacs and peonies begins. Though some **Interior/Inland gardeners** may still be experiencing snow or frost, many will be delighting in the best that spring has to offer, with late-flowering bulbs such as tulips and flowering trees such as crabapples.

THINGS TO DO

The new gardening season is upon us, one where we haven't forgotten to weed or water, where all our plants are properly spaced and well staked, and where no insects have chewed any leaves. Now is the time for **Interior/Inland gardeners** to finish tidying up the garden, preparing the garden beds and getting the planting done. **Coastal gardeners** are staking floppy plants, pinching back perennials and thinning out direct-sown plants.

MAY

8

9

Coastal gardeners should continue
to prune early-blooming trees and shrubs
as they finish flowering.

10

11

Interior/Inland gardeners can move
or divide any perennials that didn't have
enough space last summer.

12

13

14

Clematis such as C. 'Gravetye Beauty' (*left*) is a popular
perennial vine with beautiful, showy flowers in many
shapes and sizes. By planting several varieties, you
can have clematis in bloom from spring to fall.

Clockwise from top right: Clematis 'Hagley Hybrid';
Clematis 'Etoile Violette'; wisteria over archway

ALL GARDENS

By now on the **Coast**, and by the end of the month in the **Interior/Inland**, you will have a good idea of what has been damaged or killed over winter, and you can trim back or remove plants as necessary.

When planning your vegetable garden, consider planting extra to donate to a local food bank or homeless shelter. Even if you just end up with the inevitable extra zucchini and tomatoes, they can be put to good use.

May is the perfect time to plant such vegetables as beets, leaf lettuce, peas, radishes, potatoes and spinach. They are easy to grow from seed and mature by mid- to late summer.

COAST

Plant tender transplants such as pumpkins, tomatoes, begonias and coleus. Water newly planted plants during extended dry periods.

Pull weeds as you see them sprout to prevent a much bigger weeding job later.

INTERIOR/INLAND

Clear away any of the annuals or vegetables that didn't make it to the compost pile last fall.

Work compost into your garden beds and fork them over, removing weeds as you go, to prepare them for planting.

MAY

15

16

Coastal gardeners *should plant annuals that prefer drier weather and vegetables that need warmer weather now to fill in where spring bloomers are fading.*

17

18

Interior/Inland gardeners *should prune early-flowering shrubs, such as forsythia, once they are finished flowering, if needed.*

19

20

21

Plant a sunny spring perennial such as leopard's bane (*left*) with tulips and forget-me-nots to create a cheerful April–May display; a healthy lawn (*top right*)

TURFGRASS

Turfgrass aficionados are having a hard time these days. Many cities are taking steps to ban pesticide use on lawns, and summer water bans leave turf dry and crisp during hot spells. Alternative groundcovers and xeriscapes are being hailed as the way of the future, but there are positives to turfgrasses that make them worth keeping. Lawns efficiently filter pollutants out of run-off water, prevent soil erosion, retain moisture, cool the air and resist drought.

It is possible to have a healthy, attractive organic lawn. Grass is an extremely competitive plant, capable of fighting off invasions by weeds, pests and diseases without the use of chemicals. Watering with compost tea, for example, encourages a healthy lawn and increases pest and disease resistance.

Although lawns require a layer of thatch to improve wear tolerance, reduce compaction and insulate against weather extremes, too thick a thatch layer can prevent water absorption, make the grass susceptible to heat, drought and cold and encourage pest and disease problems. De-thatch lawns in spring only when the thatch layer is more than ³/₄" (2 cm) deep.

The official last frost date generally falls between February 28 and May 31, depending on the year and where you live. Judge the planting by how the year is progressing. In a warm year, when nights stay above freezing well before the last frost date, you can put in a few tender plants, such as tomatoes. You may gain several weeks on the growing season. In a cool year, you may have to wait until after the last frost date to give the soil more time to warm before planting tender heat-lovers such as beans (*left*).

MAY

22

23

Interior/Inland gardeners can begin
to harden off any houseplants that
will be moved outdoors for summer.

24

25

Coastal gardeners should top up
mulch to suppress weeds and keep
roots cool and moist.

26

27

28

With their wide variety of leaf
shapes, sizes and colors, hostas
(left) are a popular addition to
shaded gardens.

Here are some tips for maintaining a healthy, organic lawn:

- Aerate your lawn in spring, after active growth begins, to relieve compaction and allow water and air to move freely through the soil.

- Feed the soil, not the plants. Organic fertilizers or compost will encourage a healthy population of soil microbes. These work with roots to provide plants with nutrients and to fight off attacks by pests and diseases. Apply an organic fertilizer in late spring after you aerate the lawn and in fall just as the grass goes dormant.

- Mow lawns to a height of 2–2 ½" (5–6 cm). If kept this height, the remaining leaf blade will shade the ground, preventing moisture loss, keeping roots cooler, reducing the stress the grass suffers from being mowed and helping the grass out-compete weeds for space and sun-light.

May-blooming flowers: (*clockwise from top*) irises are one of the last spring bloomers in **Coastal gardens** while bergenia is heralding spring in the coldest **Interior/Inland gardens**; rockcress, phlox and heather flowers attact bees & butterflies and look exceptional in rock gardens.

MAY

29

30

31

Interior/Inland gardeners can continue to
harden off early-started seedlings and
purchased plants so they will be ready to plant
outside when the weather is warm enough.

Though sometimes considered invasive, forget-me-
nots (*left*) are easy-to-grow, reliable bloomers and
perfect for beginning gardeners, as are rockcress
(*top right*) and basket-of-gold (*bottom right*) .

- Grass clippings should be left on the lawn to return their nutrients to the soil and add organic matter. Mowing your lawn once a week or as often as needed during the vigorous growing season will ensure that the clippings decompose quickly.

- Healthy turfgrass will out-compete most weeds. Remove weeds by hand. If you must use chemicals, apply them only to the weeds. Chemical herbicides disrupt the balance of soil microbes and are not necessary to have a healthy lawn.

Accept that grass will not grow everywhere. Grass requires plenty of sun and regular moisture. Many trees and buildings provide too much shade and don't allow enough water to penetrate the soil for grass to grow successfully. Use mulch or other groundcovers in areas where you have trouble growing grass. When selecting trees to plant in the lawn, choose ones that will provide only light shade and that will enjoy the plentiful water they will be sharing with the grass, or have a grass-free zone extending from the base of the tree to the dripline.

Lawns need very little water to remain green. Watering deeply and infrequently will encourage deep roots that are not easily damaged during periods of drought. Generally a quarter inch (5 mm) of water per week will keep grass alive and 1" (2.5 cm) per week will keep it green.

JUNE

*The long, warm days
of summer are with us, and the
garden flourishes.*

JUNE

1

2

*In **Interior/Inland gardens**, heat-loving plants such as beans and marigolds will germinate quickly in the warm soil. Direct sow early in June.*

3

4

Water transplants regularly until they become established.

5

6

7

Cranesbill geraniums (*left*) are charming late-spring flowers with attractive foliage. The leaves of some species emit a lemon-mint scent.

Impatiens and ageratum (*top right*) in a tower planter; daylilies (*bottom right*) planted en masse serve as a screen

In June, the grass is green, flowerbeds are filling and perennials, trees and shrubs are blooming. We watch as seeds germinate and leaves unfold. The soil is warm enough for even the most tender plants. All gardeners are watching for dry spells when young and newly planted gardens may need extra water.

THINGS TO DO

June is the month to finish up the planting and begin the general maintenance work that will keep larger projects to a minimum.

ALL GARDENS

Apply mulch to shrub, perennial and vegetable beds. Doing so will shade the roots and reduce the amount of water the plants will require.

Pinch late-flowering perennials back lightly to encourage bushier growth and more flowers.

Identify the insects you find in your garden. You may be surprised to find out how many are beneficial.

If you notice signs of pests or disease (spots, wilted leaves, webbing or holes in blooms) take a sample to a local greenhouse or testing facility for identification, and control and prevention measures.

Pull weeds out of beds when you see them to avoid having to spend an entire day doing it later. A regular weeding regime keeps weeds under control.

Watch for the early signs of pest and disease problems. They are easiest to deal with when they are just beginning.

Remove dead flowers from plants growing in tubs, window boxes and hanging baskets. Deadheading encourages more flowering and keeps displays looking tidy.

JUNE

8

9

Coastal gardeners should trim hedges if needed. Keep the tops a bit narrower than the bases to allow light to penetrate evenly.

10

11

If you haven't done so already, clean out your water garden.

12

13

14

Despite the delicate look of its satiny flowers, godetia (*left*) enjoys the cooler weather of spring and early summer. Plants often die back as the summer progresses.

Clockwise from top right: bee balm; black-eyed Susans mixed with purple coneflower; purple coneflower; artemisia; catmint

Perennials to pinch back:

- Artemisia (*Artemisia species*)
- Bee Balm (*Monarda didyma*)
- Black-eyed Susan (*Rudbeckia* species)
- Catmint (*Nepeta* hybrids)
- Purple Coneflower (*Echinacea purpurea*)
- Shasta Daisy (*Leucanthemum* hybrids)

15

16

Interior/Inland gardeners **can plant** *tender transplants such as pumpkins, tomatoes, begonias and coleus.*

17

18

Stake plants before they fill in if you haven't already done so.

19

20

21

Coreopsis (*left*) enlivens a summer garden with its bright yellow, continuous blooms. Shear back in late summer for more flowers in fall.

Clockwise from top right: flowering maple in a container; charming container garden display; million bells with bidens

COAST

Pinch off the faded flowerheads from rhododendrons and azaleas as they finish flowering. Next year's flowers are formed soon after and will be more impressive if the plants are not spending energy producing seeds pods from this year's flowers.

Remove spring-flowering annuals such as pansies, annual candytuft, lobelia and clarkia as they fade in the summer. Replace them with summer blooming annuals like ageratum, black-eyed Susan, California poppy, marigold and nasturtium.

INTERIOR/INLAND

Prune early-flowering shrubs that have finished flowering to encourage the development of young shoots that will bear flowers the following year.

Many houseplants enjoy spending the summer outside in a shady location. The brighter a location required for your plant indoors, the more likely it is to do well outdoors. Avoid putting plants in direct sun because they will have a hard time adjusting to the weaker intensity and lower level of light when they are moved indoors at the end of the summer.

JUNE

22

23

Consider mixing different plants together in a container. You can create contrasts of color, texture and habit and give a small garden an inviting appearance.

24

25

Interior/Inland gardeners *should replace early vegetable crops such as spinach with heat-loving beans. There will still be plenty of time for them to mature before fall.*

26

27

28

The flowers of *Salvia farinacea* 'Victoria' (*left*) are a beautiful deep violet blue. They look stunning planted with yellow or orange flowers such as nasturtiums, California poppies or marigolds.

Clockwise from top right: marigolds, sweet potato vine and begonias in planters; a deck improved by a vibrant container garden; browallia, sweet potato vine, morning glory, dahlia and coleus in pots; flowering maple with petunias and vinca

CONTAINER GARDENING

Most plants can be grown in containers. Annuals, perennials, vegetables, shrubs and even trees can be adapted to container culture.

There are many advantages to gardening in containers:

- They work well in small spaces. Even apartment dwellers with small balconies can enjoy the pleasures of gardening with planters on the balcony.

- They are mobile. Containers can be moved around to take advantage of light or shade and can even be moved into a sheltered location for winter.

- They are easier to reach. Container plantings allow people in wheelchairs or with back problems to garden without having to bend a lot.

- They are useful for extending the season. You can get an early start without the transplant shock that many plants suffer when moved outdoors. You can also protect plants from an early frost in fall.

Put trailing plants near the edge of a container to spill out, and bushy and upright plants in the middle where they will give height and depth to the planting.

Coastal gardeners should prune wisteria right after blooming to encourage flowering all summer long.

Water gardens can be created in containers. Many ready-made container gardens are available, or you can create your own. Garden centers have lots of water garden supplies, and many water plants will grow as well in a large tub as they will in a pond.

Though considered old-fashioned by some gardeners, petunias (*left*) are versatile and dependable annuals that bloom continuously in any sunny location. New varieties of this flower seem to appear every spring in local greenhouses.

Spirea (*top right*) by water feature

Most perennials, shrubs or trees will require more winter protection in containers than they would if grown in the ground. Because the roots are above ground level, they are exposed to the winter wind and cycles of freezing and thawing. Protect container-grown plants by insulating the inside of the container. Thin sheets of foam insulation can be purchased and fitted around the inside of the pot before the soil is added. Containers can also be moved to sheltered locations. Garden sheds and unheated garages work well to protect plants from the cold and wind of winter.

Gardeners can get more than a month's head start on the gardening season by using containers. Tomatoes, pumpkins and watermelons can be started from seed a month before you would traditionally plant them outdoors. Plant them in large containers so they can be moved outside during warm days and brought back in at night as needed until they can be left out overnight. Doing this prevents the stretching that many early-started plants suffer from if kept indoors for too long before being planted into the garden.

Evergreens can be pruned once the new growth has fully extended, but while it is still tender. This new growth is called a "candle" (*right*). Each candle can be pinched back by up to half to encourage bushier growth. Never cut conifers back into old wood because most species cannot regenerate from old wood.

JULY

The hot, sunny days of July encourage us
to sit back, relax and enjoy all the hard
work we've put into our gardens.

July

1

2

*Tie new shoots of climbing vines
such as morning glory and sweet peas
to their supports.*

3

4

*Use an organic fertilizer on container plants
and on garden plants if compost is scarce.*

5

6

7

The tender rose 'Ainsley Dickson' (*left*) is a reliable
repeat bloomer in late summer if planted in full sun.
It can produce up to 120 blossoms in its first season.

A riot of phlox, daylilies, yarrow, ageratum and snapdragons (*top right*); a natural-looking water
feature (*bottom right*)

Flowerbeds have filled in, green tomatoes ripen on the vine. The season's transplants are established and need less frequent watering. By July, the days are long and warm. The garden appears to grow before your eyes. Some plants can't take the heat and fall dormant while others thrive and fill in the spaces left behind.

THINGS TO DO

Heat and drought can spell disaster for your lawn and garden if you haven't followed good watering practices. Water bans are common in many communities, and frequent, shallow watering earlier in the season creates problems in July when roots unaccustomed to searching deeply for water suffer in its absence.

ALL GARDENS

Water deeply, but no more than once a week during dry spells. Water early in the day to minimize potential disease and reduce water lost through evaporation. Watering late in the day can promote the development of mildew and mold on some plants.

Pick zucchini when they are small and at their tender and tasty best. Consider donating any extra vegetables to a homeless shelter or food bank, where they will be much appreciated.

To ensure the survival of a new plant in your garden, find out what its optimum growing conditions are, and then plant it where these conditions exist in your yard. For example, don't plant a shrub that needs full sun in a north-facing location.

If daytime temperatures are hot, water your container plants at least once a day.

JULY

8

9

Weed regularly to keep beds tidy.

10

11

Thin vegetable crops such as beets, carrots and turnips. Crowded plants lead to poor crops.

Top up water gardens regularly if levels drop because of evaporation.

12

13

14

Annual clary sage (*left*) loves sun, and its brilliantly colored bracts attract butterflies and hummingbirds to the flowers. Plant it among other sun-loving annuals and perennials where its whites, pinks and purples will provide bright bursts of color.

Clockwise from top right: violas; statice; bachelor's buttons

COAST

Deadhead perennials and annuals as needed to keep them blooming. Remove foliage that was damaged by slugs in the spring. Trim back early blooming perennials to encourage new foliage growth.

Pick herbs at the prime of their growth to dry for use in winter.

INTERIOR/INLAND

Trim hedges regularly to keep them looking tidy and lush.

Pick peas, beans and tomatoes as soon as they are ripe to encourage the plants to produce more. As pea vines begin to die back, pull up the plants, and consider a second crop of another fast-maturing vegetable such as radishes, or plant flowering annuals such as marigolds and nasturtiums to fill in the gaps.

Plan to replace fading flowers and vegetables by sowing seeds for a fall display or crop. Peas, bush beans, annual candytuft and lobelia are often finished fruiting or blooming by mid- to late summer, leaving holes in the garden that can be filled by new plants. Seeds for replacement plants can be direct sown or started indoors.

JULY

15

16

Top mulch up if it is getting thin in places in your garden. Mulch protects roots, holds in moisture and helps keep weeds at bay.

17

18

Continue to tie plants to their stakes as they grow.

19

20

Heliopsis (*left*), a native prairie perennial, is easy to grow and tolerates poor conditions, though it thrives in full sun and fertile, moist soil. Its name means 'resembling the sun' and its sun-like blooms make long-lasting cut flowers.

Use a mixture of annuals and perennials to create garden rooms that add privacy or create paths through the garden (*opposite*).

21

GARDEN PROBLEMS

Chewed leaves, mildews and nutrient deficiencies tend to become noticeable in July when plants finish their first flush of growth and turn their attention to flowering and fruiting.

Such problems can be minimized if you develop a good problem management program. Though it may seem complicated, problem management is a simple process that relies on correct and timely identification of the problem, then using the least environmentally harmful method to deal with it.

JULY

22

23

Turn the compost pile, and when the compost is ready, add it to your flowerbeds and vegetable garden.

24

25

Trim or shear back early-flowering perennials when they have finished blooming.

26

27

28

'Cupcake' (*left*) is a delightful miniature rose with a classic hybrid tea shape. It produces an abundance of blooms and is disease resistant.

Clockwise from top right: deer-pruned cedars; a swallowtail on cherry blossoms; a birdbath in a shade garden

Garden problems fall into three basic categories:

- pests, including mollusks such as slugs and snails, insects such as aphids, codling moths, nematodes and whiteflies, and mammals such as mice, rabbits, raccoons and deer

- diseases, caused by bacteria, fungi and viruses

- physiological problems, caused by nutrient deficiencies, too much or too little water and incorrect light levels.

Choose healthy plants that have been developed for their resistance to common problems and that will perform well in the conditions provided by your garden.

Prevention is the most important aspect of problem management. A healthy garden resists problems and develops a natural balance between beneficial and harmful organisms.

JULY

29

30

Coastal gardeners can start seeds now for plants that will enjoy the cool, moist weather of fall.

31

Cup-and-saucer vine (*below*) produces sweetly scented flowers that are cream colored when they emerge and turn purple as they age.

Ladybird beetle (*top right*), a beneficial insect that feasts on aphids; Dahlberg daisies (*bottom right*)

PEST CONTROL

Correct identification of problems is the key to solving them. Just because an insect is on a plant doesn't mean it's doing any harm.

- Cultural controls are the day-to-day gardening techniques you use to keep your garden healthy. Weed, mulch, keep tools clean and grow problem-resistant cultivars to keep your garden healthy.

- Physical controls are the hands-on part of problem solving. Picking insects off leaves, removing diseased foliage and creating barriers to stop rabbits from getting into the vegetable patch are examples of physical controls.

- Biological controls use natural and introduced populations of predators that prey on pests. Birds, snakes, frogs, spiders, some insects and even bacteria naturally feed on some problem insects. Soil microbes work with plant roots to increase their resistance to disease.

Chemical pest control should always be a last resort. There are many alternatives that pose no danger to gardeners or their families and pets.

For strong, pest-resistant plants, try watering them with compost tea. Compost Tea Recipe: Mix a shovelful of compost in a 5-gallon (20-liter) bucket of water or a bucketful of compost in a 45-gallon (170-liter) barrel of water and let sit for a week. Dilute this mix, preferably with rainwater or filtered water, until it resembles weak tea.

The pesticide industry has responded to consumer demand for effective, environmentally safe pest control products. Biopesticides are made from plant, animal, bacterial or mineral sources. They are effective in small quantities and decompose quickly in the environment. These products may help us reduce our reliance on chemical pesticides.

AUGUST

*Sit back and relax; the ripening fruit,
vegetables and seeds are signs that summer
is nearing its end.*

AUGUST

1

2

Continue to deadhead perennials and annuals to keep the blooms coming.

3

4

Pick apples as soon as they are ready, being careful not to bruise the fruit.

5

6

7

Calendula (*left*) is an easy flower to grow from seed. It blooms quickly in spring and all summer long, even tolerating light frost. It can be used as a culinary herb as well.

Clockwise from top right: geraniums; apples; petunias

The warm days of July blend into August, but the nights are cooler. If it hasn't been too dry, many plants we might have given up on revive and begin a late display of color.

THINGS TO DO

The garden seems to take care of itself in August. Gardeners putter about, tying up floppy hollyhock spikes, picking vegetables and pulling an odd weed, but the frenzy of early summer is over and we take the time just to sit and enjoy the results of our labors.

ALL GARDENS

Watch for pests that may be planning to hibernate in the debris around your plants or the bark of your trees. Taking care of a few insects now may keep several generations out of your garden next summer.

Continue to water during dry spells. Plants shouldn't need deep watering more than once a week at this time of the year.

Turn the layers of the compost pile and continue to add garden soil, kitchen scraps and garden debris not diseased or infested with insects.

Avoid pruning rust-prone plants such as mountain ash and crabapple in late summer and fall because many rusts are releasing spores now.

Gradually move houseplants that have been summering outdoors into shadier locations so they will be prepared for the lower light levels indoors. Make sure they aren't infested with bugs; the pests will be harder to control once the plants are indoors.

8

9

Container gardens will need to be watered twice as often because plant roots will be filling the pots by this time in the season.

10

11

Continue watering newly planted perennials, trees and shrubs. Water deeply to encourage root growth.

12

13

14

The French marigold (*left*) is just one variety of this popular annual. All marigolds are low-maintenance plants that stand up well to heat, wind and rain.

COAST

Place orders for spring-flowering bulbs or purchase from garden centers so you will have them ready to plant this fall.

There is still time to plant a crop of fast-maturing flowers and vegetables. Choose those that will thrive in the cooler, wetter weather of fall. Imagine eating fresh salad greens such as kale, arugula and sorrel in October or November.

INTERIOR/INLAND

Remove worn-out annuals and vegetables, and replace them with the ones you started last month. Shearing some annuals and perennials back will encourage new growth, giving them a fresh look for fall.

Reduce fertilizer applications to allow perennials, shrubs and trees ample time to harden off before the cold weather.

Plants such as Siberian bugloss (top), anemone (top right), lupins (center) and liatrus (right) are good plants to divide if you're just starting your perennial collection. They recover and fill in quickly when divided.

AUGUST

15

16

Interior/Inland gardeners should find a source of straw for mulch now because it can be harder to find later in fall.

17

18

Coastal gardeners should visit their garden centers this month. Many centers will be selling pansies, mums, flowering cabbage and kale. Plant these to add some new color to a fading garden.

19

20

Zinnias (*below*) are easy to grow, come in a rainbow of colors and make long-lasting cut flowers for floral arrangements.

Clockwise from top right: hydrangea, sedum and aster are easy to propagate from stem cuttings.

21

PLANT PROPAGATION

August is a good time to propagate plants. Taking cuttings and gathering seed are great ways to increase your plant collection and to share some of your favorite plants with friends and family.

Now is a good time to divide some perennials and to note which of your plants will need dividing next spring. Look for these signs that perennials need dividing:

- The center of the plant has died out.

- The plant is no longer flowering as profusely as it did in previous years.

- The plant is encroaching on the growing space of other plants.

Perennials, trees, shrubs and tender perennials that are treated like annuals can all be started from cuttings. This method is an excellent way to propagate varieties and cultivars that you really like but that are slow or difficult to start from seed or that don't produce viable seed.

The easiest cuttings to take from woody plants such as trees, shrubs and vines are called semi-ripe, semi-mature or semi-hardwood cuttings. They are taken from mature new growth that has not become completely woody yet, usually in late summer or early fall.

AUGUST

22

23

Stop fertilizing roses four to six weeks before the first frost to avoid damaging late lush growth.

24

25

26

27

28

You won't need to collect seed from borage (*left*) because these plants self-seed profusely and will no doubt turn up in your garden next spring.

Clockwise from top right: evening primrose; nasturtiums with creeping Jenny; zinnias

The easiest way to start is to collect seeds of annual plants in your own garden. Choose plants that are not hybrids or the seeds will probably not come true to type and may not germinate at all. A few easy plants to collect from are

- Calendula (*Calendula officinalis*)
- Coriander (*Coriandrum sativum*)
- Evening Primrose (*Oenothera biennis*)
- Fennel (*Foeniculum vulgare*)
- Marigold (*Tagetes* species and hybrids)
- Nasturtium (*Tropaeolum majus*)
- Poppy (*Papaver rhoeas*)
- Zinnia (*Zinnia elegans*)

There is some debate over what size cuttings should be. Some people claim that smaller cuttings are more likely to root and will root more quickly. Others claim that larger cuttings develop more roots and become established more quickly once planted. Try different sizes and see what works best for you.

Always make cuttings just below a leaf node (the point where the leaves are attached to the stem).

Many gardeners enjoy the hobby of collecting and planting seed. You need to know a few basic things before you begin:

- Know your plant. Correctly identify the plant and learn about its life cycle. You will need to know when it flowers, when the seeds are likely to ripen and how the plant disperses its seeds in order to collect them.

- Find out if there are special requirements for starting the seeds. For example, do they need a hot or cold period to germinate?

29

30

Seeds of different species have different shelf lives. Check seed catalogues or seed packages for information on how long different seeds will last.

31

Nasturtiums (*below*) are versatile annuals. Their edible flowers and foliage are attractive additions to baskets and containers as well as to salads. Even the seedpods can be pickled and used as a substitute for capers.

Clockwise from top right: drying poppy seed-heads; Oriental poppy; golden clematis flowers and seedheads

When collecting seed, consider the following:

- Collect seeds once they are ripe but before they are shed from the parent plant.

- Remove capsules, heads or pods as they begin to dry and remove the seeds later, once they are completely dry.

- Place a paper bag over a seedhead as it matures and loosely tie it in place to collect seeds as they are shed.

- Dry seeds after they've been collected. Place them on a paper-lined tray and leave them in a warm, dry location for one to three weeks.

- Separate seeds from the other plant parts and clean them before storing.

- Store seeds in air-tight containers in a cool, frost-free location.

Don't collect seeds from the wild because wild harvesting is severely depleting many plant populations. Many species and populations of wild plants are protected, and it is illegal to collect their seeds.

Depending on the size of your perennials, you can divide them using a shovel or pitchfork (for large plants), a sharp knife (for small plants) or your hands (for easily divided plants).

Collecting and saving seeds is a time-honored tradition. Early settlers brought seeds with them when they came to North America and saved them carefully each fall for the following spring.

SEPTEMBER

Though the warm weather continues for most gardeners, some are seeing the end of summer and even a first frost or snow.

SEPTEMBER

1

2

Don't cut back ornamental grasses in the fall. Leave the stalks on the plant to protect the crown. Prune back in spring.

3

4

Keep asters and other fall bloomers well watered to prevent powdery mildew.

5

6

7

Strawflower (*left*), amaranthus (*top right*), goldenrod (*center right*) and bluebeard (*bottom right*) can be harvested now for dried flower arrangements.

Leaves may begin to change color, ripening seedheads nod in the breeze and brightly colored berries and fruit adorn many trees and shrubs. This is usually quite a dry month for **Coastal gardens** while **Interior/Inland gardens** enjoy the revival of many plants with the cooler nights.

THINGS TO DO

Having enjoyed another summer garden, some of the fall clean-up begins.

ALL GARDENS

Take advantage of end-of-season sales. Many garden centers are getting rid of trees, shrubs and perennials at reduced prices. There is still plenty of time for the roots to become established before the ground freezes. Do not buy plants that are excessively pot-bound.

If you've let your weeds get out of hand over summer, be sure to pull them up before they set seed to avoid having even more weeds popping up in the garden next summer. Avoid tossing weeds that have gone to seed into your compost heap. If your compost isn't hot enough, the seeds will germinate when you add the compost to your garden.

Many people falsely associate goldenrod flowers (above) with hayfever. The inconspicuous flowers of ragweed, which blooms at the same time, are actually responsible.

SEPTEMBER

8

9

Set up birdfeeders and begin to feed the birds if you didn't do so all summer.

10

11

Check houseplants for insect pests before moving them back indoors for winter.

12

13

14

Bigleaf hydrangea (*left*) is a popular shrub but needs a very protected site and moist soil to survive in Interior or Inland gardens.

Clockwise from top left: the fall colors and features of Virginia creeper, burning bush, full moon maple and ginkgo

INTERIOR/INLAND

Many annuals are undamaged by early frosts and continue to bloom until the first hard freeze.

Plant colorful fall ornamentals, such as chrysanthemums, flowering cabbage and flowering kale, available in fall at most garden centers.

Move tender container plants into a sheltered location when frost is expected. This strategy will allow you to enjoy them for longer.

The changing colors are a sure sign that fall is here. Bright reds, golds, bronzes and coppers seem to give warmth to a cool day. The display doesn't have to be reserved for a walk in the park. Include trees and shrubs with good fall color such as those listed here to your garden:

- Burning Bush (*Euonymus alatus*)
- Cotoneaster (*Cotoneaster*)
- Maples (*Acer*)
- Virginia Creeper (*Parthenocissus quinquefolia*)
- Witch-hazel (*Hamamelis*)

SEPTEMBER

15

16

Interior/Inland gardeners should pull out annual plants and vegetables as they fade or are killed by frost.

17

18

Continue to water the garden during dry spells. Consistent watering in fall helps prepare plants for winter.

19

20

The cheery golden marguerite daisy plant (*below*) forms a tidy mound that works wonderfully in both formal and informal garden settings.

Clockwise from top right: alliums; tulips, bluebells and candytuft; black-eyed Susan; tulips and primroses

21

When planting bulbs, you may want to add a little bonemeal to the soil to encourage root development.

COAST

Once the rainy weather returns, plant out trees and shrubs that need more moisture to survive than they would receive in summer. The cool, moist weather of fall will encourage root growth.

Begin to plant bulbs for a great display next spring. Tulips, daffodils, crocuses, scillas, muscaris and alliums are just a few of the bulbs whose flowers will welcome you back into the garden next year.

Spring-flowering perennials such as primroses and candytuft can be planted now. They will be a delightful sight in a few short months.

SEPTEMBER

22

23

Coastal gardeners should clean up the debris around pest- and disease-prone plants such as apples to reduce overwintering populations.

24

Coastal gardeners should direct sow perennial seeds, such as astilbe, columbine and delphinium, which need cold treatment to sprout. Mark their location because they will not germinate until spring. They can also be planted in containers and placed in a cold frame during winter.

25

26

27

28

Echinacea purpurea (*left*), commonly called purple coneflower and used as a popular herbal cold remedy, is a long-blooming, drought-resistant perennial. Its distinctively cone-shaped flowers look good in fresh and dried floral arrangements.

CREATING WILDLIFE HABITAT

The rapid and relentless rate of urban sprawl has led to the loss of wildlife habitat.Our gardens can easily provide some of the space, shelter, food and water that wildlife needs. Though we may not want to attract every creature, we can make at least some wildlife welcome in our gardens. Here are a few tips for attracting wildlife to your garden:

- Make sure at least some of the plants in your garden are locally native. Birds and small mammals are accustomed to certain plants for food. These plants will attract wildlife to your garden, where the animals may be tempted to try some of the other fruit that is not native.

- Provide a source of water. A pond with a shallow side or a birdbath will offer water for drinking and bathing. Frogs and toads eat a wide variety of insect pests and will happily take up residence in or near a ground-level water feature.

- A variety of birdfeeders and seed will encourage different species of birds to visit your garden. Some birds will visit an elevated feeder, but others prefer a feeder set at or near ground level. Fill your feeders regularly—once you start to feed the birds, they will come to depend on you as a source of food.

Garden features such as birdbaths and birdfeeders *(top left)* and tall flowering perennials such as bee balm, coneflower and yarrow *(top right)* attract wildlife to your yard.

SEPTEMBER

29

Cool fall weather is ideal for sowing grass seed and repairing thin patches in the lawn.

30

The zinnia (*below*) is named after Johann Gottfried Zinn (1727–59), a German botany professor who started growing these South American flowers from seed in Europe.

Clockwise from top right: birdfeeder; bee balm with butterfly; sunflower; flycatcher on a cherry tree

Shelter is the final aspect to keeping your resident wildlife happy. Patches of dense shrubs, tall grasses and mature trees provide shelter. As well, you can leave a small pile of twiggy brush in an out-of-the-way place. Nature stores and many garden centers sell toad houses and birdhouses.

It is a good idea to collect fallen fruit because it may attract unwanted wildlife, such as rats, skunks, raccoons and coyotes, to your garden.

Butterflies, hummingbirds and a wide variety of predatory insects will be attracted if you include lots of pollen-producing plants in your garden. Plants such as goldenrod, comfrey, bee balm, salvia, Joe Pye weed, black-eyed Susan, catmint, purple coneflower, coreopsis, hollyhock and yarrow will attract pollen lovers.

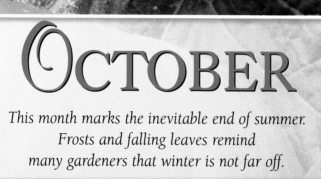

OCTOBER

This month marks the inevitable end of summer.
Frosts and falling leaves remind
many gardeners that winter is not far off.

OCTOBER

1

2

*Continue to plant bulbs. They need to get
a bit of root growth in fall in order
to flower next spring.*

3

4

*Faded annuals and vegetables can be pulled
up and added to the compost pile.*

5

6

7

If the first frost hasn't yet arrived and your apples are still
on the tree (left), now is the time to harvest them.
However, some varieties taste better after the first
frost, so you may want to wait to pick these.

Clockwise from top right: maple tree;
a bountiful harvest of carrots;
endearing teddy bear sunflowers

Most gardens are still vigorous in early October, but by Halloween, many gardens are looking withered as all but the hardiest flowers in **Interior/Inland gardens** are bitten by frost, and the rain on the **Coast** has dampened the spirits of many late-season bloomers.

THINGS TO DO

October is the time to tidy up and start putting the garden to bed for another year.

ALL GARDENS

When raking leaves in fall, you can use them in different ways: add them to the compost pile; gather them into their own compost pile to decompose into leaf mould; or mow them over and then pile them onto flowerbeds. Whole leaves can become matted together, encouraging fungal disease.

Cure winter squash, such as acorn squash, pumpkins and spaghetti squash, in a cool, frost-free location before storing for winter.

Dig up tuberous tender plants such as begonias for drying and storing over winter.

Unless your plants have been afflicted with some sort of disease, you can leave faded perennial growth in place and clean it up in spring. The stems will collect leaves and snow, protecting the roots and crown of the plant over the winter.

OCTOBER

8

9

On the Coast, *water newly planted trees, shrubs and perennials if rainfall is inconsistent or insufficient.*

10

11

In **Interior/Inland areas,** *continue to mow the lawn if needed, but don't mow frozen blades of grass. Wait for frost to melt off and dry before cutting the grass.*

12

13

14

The serviceberry (*left*) is a small tree that bears white flowers and edible red berries in spring and lovely orange-red foliage in fall. It requires little maintenance and does quite well near water.

Fall is a great time to improve your soil. Amendments added now can be worked in lightly. By planting time next spring, the amendments will have been further worked in by the actions of worms and other soil microorganisms and by the freezing and thawing that takes place over winter.

Local farmers' markets are often the best places to find a wide variety of seasonal vegetables and flowers (*above and below*) or to get growing ideas for spring.

COAST

Some perennials can be divided now. Mid- to late summer bloomers will probably flower next summer if divided now. Avoid dividing spring and early-summer bloomers because the shock of division may prevent them from flowering next year.

Some hardy greens and root crops can be harvestd late, for example, cabbage, kale, broccoli, carrots and turnips.

Cover tomato plants to keep them dry. This prevents blight from killing them.

INTERIOR/INLAND

Harvest any remaining vegetables. Soft fruit such as tomatoes and zucchini should be harvested before the first frost, but cool-weather vegetables such as carrots, cabbage, brussels sprouts and turnips can wait a while longer because they are frost hardy.

Start mulching the garden, but avoid covering plants completely until the ground has frozen. Doing so prevents plants from rotting and deters small rodents from digging down and feasting on plant roots and crowns.

OCTOBER

15

16

Interior/Inland gardeners should
continue to tidy up dead plant material.
Most can be composted, but it's better
to throw out diseased material.

17

18

On the Coast, if there were any plants you
saw over the summer that you wanted to
try, you may be able to purchase them at a
discount now or get divisions from friends.

19

20

21

Honeysuckle vine (*left*) flowers from summer to fall
frost. Prune in spring to cut back dead growth as
new leaves emerge.

Composting (*far right*); delicious vegetables
harvested from the garden (*near right*)

COMPOSTING

One of the best additives for any type of soil is compost. Compost can be purchased at most garden centers, and many communities now have composting programs. You can easily make compost in your own garden. Though garden refuse and vegetable scraps from your kitchen left in a pile will eventually decompose, it is possible to produce compost more quickly. Here are a few suggestions for making compost:

- Compost decomposes most quickly when there is a balance between dry and fresh materials. There should be more dry matter (chopped straw or shredded leaves) than green matter (vegetable scraps and grass clippings).

- Layer the dry and the green matter, and mix in some garden soil or previously finished compost. This step introduces decomposer organisms to the pile.

- Compost won't decompose properly if it is too wet or too dry. Keep the pile covered during heavy rain, and sprinkle it with water if it is too dry. The correct level of moisture can best be described as that of a wrung-out sponge.

22

23

Coastal gardeners should not prune back a hardy fuschia in fall because that will kill the plant. Prune in spring.

24

25

In **Interior/Inland areas** continue to water trees and shrubs until freeze up. Apply an organic anti-desiccant to newly planted evergreens to reduce winter moisture loss.

26

27

28

Yarrow's showy, flat-topped flower-heads (*left*) provide months of continuous color in summer, and the seedheads persist into winter.

- To aerate the compost pile, use a garden fork to poke holes in it or turn it regularly. Use a thermometer with a long probe attached, similar to a large meat thermometer, to check the temperature in your pile. When the temperature reaches 158° F (70°C), give the pile a turn.

- Finished compost is dark in color and light in texture. When you can no longer recognize what went into the compost, it is ready for use.

- Compost can be mixed into garden soil or spread on the surface as a mulch.

- If you haven't got the time or the inclination to fuss over your compost, you can just leave it in a pile, and it will eventually decompose with no added assistance from you.

- In areas with mild winters, open compost piles may attract rodents. To prevent this, store compost in a plastic bin.

Images of fall: gladiolas (*top left*); juicy clusters of vine-ripened grapes (*top*); tasty corn on the cob fresh from the garden (*above*). Many gardeners find fruiting plants to be decorative as well as useful.

OCTOBER

29

30

Coastal gardeners can mow their lawn all winter if there isn't too much snow or rain.

31

Sunflowers (*below*) are synonymous with fall for many gardeners. Their bold yellow, seed-filled flowerheads celebrate the harvest season and provide treats for the birds.

Highbush cranberry's (*Viburnum trilobum*) fall berries (*right*) attract birds and can be used to make jellies, pies and wine.

Before adding any amendments to your soil, you should get a soil test done. Simple kits to test for pH and major nutrients are available at garden centers. More thorough tests are done at government or private labs. These tests will tell you what the pH is, the comparative levels of sand, silt, clay and organic matter and the quantities of all required nutrients. They will also tell you what amendments to add and in what quantities to improve your soil.

There are other good amendments for soil, depending on what is required:

- Gypsum can be mixed into a clay soil along with compost to loosen the structure and allow water to penetrate.

- Elemental sulphur, peat moss or pine needles added on a regular basis can make an alkaline soil more acidic, especially for rhododendrons and azaleas.

- Calcitic or dolomitic limestone, hydrated lime, quicklime or wood ashes can be added to an acidic soil to make it more alkaline for lilacs and lawns.

Sunflowers (*above*) and other cut flowers can be found in abundance in farmers' markets. Use them for fresh or dried table arrangements, or flower pressing for winter crafts.

NOVEMBER

*Be it frost and snow or heavy rain,
the weather seems determined to drive us out
of the garden this month.*

NOVEMBER

1

2

Finish collecting seeds from open-pollinated flowers and vegetables. Stored in a cool, dry place, they will be ready for planting in next year's garden.

3

4

Move clay and concrete pots and statues into a protected location to prevent them from cracking over winter.

5

6

7

Annual coreopsis (*left*) self-seeds, so it may pop up from year to year in the same area if left to its own devices.

Hoarfrost (*top right*); crabapples in winter (*bottom right*)

In **Interior/Inland areas**, a few stragglers always hang on despite the inevitable frosts. Flowers such as calendula keep blooming until the ground starts to freeze, even under a light blanket of snow. The rain comes in earnest to the **Coast** and many garden plants go dormant to survive the seemingly incessant moisture.

THINGS TO DO

Garden tasks this month center around finishing tucking the garden in for winter.

ALL GARDENS

Harvest any remaining vegetables. Root vegetables, such as carrots, parsnips and turnips, and green vegetables, such as cabbages and broccoli, store well in a cool place. Their flavor is often improved after a touch of frost.

Clear away tools, hoses and garden furniture so they won't be damaged by the cold and wet weather.

Fill your birdfeeders regularly. Well-fed birds will continue to visit your garden in summer, feeding on undesirable insects in your garden.

The garden can be quite beautiful in November, especially after a light dusting of snow or frost (*above*) or when persistent fruit becomes more visible on branches (*below*).

NOVEMBER

8

9

Toss disease-free plants on the compost heap as they fade.

10

11

Coastal gardeners *may be able to harvest late-sown vegetables now. Try to pick them on a dry day to discourage the spread of fungal disease.*

12

13

The beautiful hybrid tea rose 'Rosemary Harkness' (*left*) produces fragrant orange-yellow double blooms from summer to autumn. Like other tender hybrid teas, it should be protected from harsh winter weather.

14

The richly colored rosettes of ornamental kale (*far right*) are reminiscent of roses, such as the hybrid tea 'Barbra Streisand' (*top right*).

COAST

Drought-tolerant plants can suffer from root rot during wet weather. Improve drainage to help them through the winter by growing them in raised beds.

Biennial seeds sown now will sprout and flower next summer.

Find the driest place possible to store seeds. Their rates of germination will remain highest when the seeds are kept dry. Store them in small jars to seal out moisture.

INTERIOR/INLAND

Prepare hybrid tea and other semi-hardy roses for winter before the ground freezes. Mound dirt up over the bases and cover with mulch, or cover with cardboard boxes, open the top and fill around the plants with loose, quick-drying material, such as sawdust, shredded leaves or peat moss. Hold boxes in place with a heavy rock on top when you are done.

After raking and once the lawn is dormant, apply an organic fertilizer. If you haven't needed to mow in a couple of weeks, it is probably sufficiently dormant.

Avoid completely covering perennials like this strawberry (*above*) with mulch until the ground freezes. Mound the mulch around them and store some extra mulch in a frost-free location to add once they are frozen. If you pile the mulch in the garden, you may find it has also frozen solid when you want to use it.

NOVEMBER

15

16

Coastal gardeners can continue
to harvest salad greens all winter if
they are grown in a cold frame.

17

18

Interior/Inland gardeners should spray
anti-desiccants on evergreens, such as
rhododendrons and cedars, to prevent
moisture loss over winter.

19

20

Pieris (*left*) is a beautiful plant all year long. It provides
colorful new growth in spring and summer and flowers
from late winter to mid-spring.

Clockwise from top right: hollyhock; hens and chicks;
yucca and black-eyed Susan; lilac

21

PROBLEM AREAS

If an area of your garden always seems
dry, consider a xeriscape planting in that
area. Many plants are drought resistant
and thrive even in areas that are never
watered. Black-eyed Susan, cosmos,
hollyhock, jack pine, lilac, potentilla,
prickly pear cactus, yarrow and yucca
are just a few of the many possibilities
for a dry section of the garden.

Now that you've had the chance to
observe your garden for a growing
season, consider the microclimates and
think about how you can put them to
good use. Are any areas always quick
to dry? Do some areas stay wet longer
than others? What area is the most
sheltered? Which is the least sheltered?
Cater your plantings to the microclimates of your garden.

NOVEMBER

22

23

In Interior/Inland gardens, *once the ground freezes, mound mulch around the bases of semi-hardy shrubs to protect the roots and stem bases from temperature fluctuations.*

24

25

Reduce watering and cease feeding houseplants.

26

27

28

Flowers such as marsh marigolds (*left*), astilbe (*top right*), irises (*far right*), daylilies (*center right*) and ligularia (*bottom right*) work well in damp areas of the garden because they prefer moist growing conditions.

BOG GARDENING

Turn a damp area into your own little bog garden. Dig out an area 14–20" (35–50 cm) below ground level, line with a piece of punctured pond liner and fill with soil. The area will stay wet but still allow some water to drain away, providing a perfect location to plant moisture-loving perennials. A few to consider are

- Astilbe (*Astilbe x arendsii*)
- Cardinal Flower (*Lobelia x speciosa*)
- Daylily (*Hemerocallis hybrids*)
- Doronicum (*Doronicum orientale*)
- Goat's Beard (*Aruncus dioicus*)
- Hosta (*Hosta hybrids*)
- Iris (*Iris ensata* and *I. siberica*)
- Lady's Mantle (*Alchemilla mollis*)
- Ligularia (*Ligularia dentata* and *L. wilsoniana*)
- Marsh Marigold (*Caltha palustris*)
- Meadowsweet (*Filipendula rubra* and *F. ulmaria*)
- Primrose (*Primula japonica*)
- Rodgersia (*Rodgersia aesculifolia*)

Oregon grape holly (*near right*); rock rose (*far right*); jasmine (*center right*); pieris (*bottom right*)

Rodgersia (*left*) bears bold foliage and fluffy flower plumes in mid- to late summer. It does best in a site sheltered from strong winds and extreme weather. Rodgersia plants prefer moist soil and require winter protection in colder gardens.

It is possible to grow out-of-zone plants. Reserve the warmest, most sheltered area of the garden for plants not considered fully hardy.

In **Coastal regions**, consider planting windmill palm or New Zealand flax.

In **Interior/Inland regions**, herbs and ornamental grasses are popular. Grasses add a vertical element and a bit of drama to the garden.

If you have a very exposed area in your garden, you can find plants that will do well there, or you can make a planting that will shelter the area. A hedge or group of trees or shrubs will break the wind and provide an attractive feature for your garden.

DECEMBER

Already summer seems far away.
Ghostly forms and dashes of color are all
that remain to inspire us until spring.

DECEMBER

1

2

If you have healthy willows, dogwoods, Virginia creeper or evergreens, cut a few branches to use in Christmas wreaths. Store them in a cool place until needed.

3

4

Interior/Inland gardeners *should water evergreens and shrubs thoroughly before the ground freezes. They won't have any access to water again until the ground thaws in spring.*

5

6

7

Holly (*left*) makes an attractive addition to fresh winter arrangements. To keep it looking its best, keep the cut ends consistently moist.

The garden begins its winter display of colorful and peeling bark, branches with persistent fruit and the many shades of the evergreen boughs. With a bit of luck, snow begins to pile up on **Interior/Inland** garden beds, covering withered perennials and shrubs and clinging to evergreen branches. Frosty and wet **Coastal gardens** seem to turn a deeper green, at odds with the inclement weather.

THINGS TO DO

Our thoughts turn to indoor gardening though we may still have a few garden tasks to complete before we call it a year.

ALL GARDENS

Clean tools thoroughly, and wipe them with an oily rag to prevent them from rusting before storing them for winter.

Any herbs you are growing indoors should be kept in the brightest window you have to prevent them from becoming too straggly or dying.

COAST

Lawns can be fertilized with organic fertilizer after the first frost. Use a fertilizer that promotes root growth over the winter.

Brassicas such as cabbage and brussels sprouts can often be left in the garden and harvested as needed over the winter.

Clean out your house gutters or eavestroughs to prevent winter rains from overflowing and damaging the plants below. You can add that material to your compost pile.

In December our thoughts turn to decorating for the holidays. Now is the time to use some of the flowers you dried to make potpourri, wreaths or floral arrangements (*above and left*).

DECEMBER

8

9

Interior/Inland gardeners should finish mulching the garden if they haven't already done so.

10

11

Chinese evergreen, Easter cactus, Norfolk Island pine, peacock plant, peace lily and prayer plant are among the many houseplants that tolerate low light levels.

12

13

14

Poinsettias (*left*) add rich color and beauty to our homes during the dark days of December. They are available in November and last well after Christmas has passed.

Clockwise from top right: dragon tree (*Dracaena marginata*) and Balfour aralia; *Cattleya* orchid; *Miltonopsis* orchid; cast iron plant

INTERIOR/INLAND

Gently brush snow off flexible evergreen branches. Heavy snow can weigh down upright juniper and cedar branches enough to permanently bend them downwards.

If rabbits and mice are a problem in your garden, you can protect your trees and shrubs with chicken wire. Wrap the wire around the plant bases and higher up the tree or shrub than you expect the snow to reach.

Houseplants are more than just attractive—they clean the air in our homes. Many dangerous and common toxins, such as benzene, formaldehyde and trichloroethylene, are absorbed and eliminated by houseplants.

HOUSEPLANT CARE

You don't have to forget gardening completely when the snow begins to fly. All you have to do is turn your attention to indoor gardening. Houseplants clean the air, soften the hard edges of a room and provide color, texture and interest to your home.

Just as you did for the garden outdoors, match your indoor plants to the conditions your home provides. If a room receives little light, consider houseplants that require low light levels.

15

16

Check under the eaves to make sure any plants growing there are getting enough water through the fall and winter.

17

18

Bright-light-tolerant plants include cacti, goldfish plant, jade plant and snake plant.

19

20

Although orchids are reputed to be difficult and needy, some orchids such as the moth orchid *Phalaenopsis* (*left*) are easy to grow on a windowsill. There are many thousands of species of orchids in an amazing array of sizes, shapes, colors and fragrances.

Indoor water garden (*center right*); braided lucky bamboo (*bottom right*)

21

Plants that like humid conditions, such as African violets, ferns and philodendrons may do best in your bathroom, where showering and the water in the toilet bowl maintain higher moisture levels than in any other room. Plants that tolerate or prefer dry air, such as cacti, ficus, palms and poinsettias will grow well with no added humidity.

There are three aspects of interior light to consider: intensity, duration and quality. Intensity is the difference between a south-facing window with full sun and a north-facing room with no direct sunlight. Duration is how long the light lasts in a specific location. An east-facing window will have a shorter duration of light than a south-facing window. Quality refers to the spectrum of the light. Natural light provides a broader spectrum than artificial light.

Watering is a key element to houseplant care. Over-watering can be as much of a problem as under-watering. As you did with your garden plants, water thoroughly and infrequently. Let the soil dry out a bit before watering plants. Some plants are the exception to this rule. Find out what the water requirements of your houseplants are so you will have an idea of how frequently or infrequently you will need to water.

Look for creative ways to display your plants and add beauty to your home. Indoor fountains and moisture-loving plants, such as a peace lily in a vase of water (*top*), are interesting and attractive. They add a decorative touch to a houseplant display.

DECEMBER

22

23

Amaryllis can be enjoyed indoors at this time of year. When it's finished blooming, cut off the flower stem (but not the leaves) and keep the soil moist, and it may bloom a second time the same winter.

24

25

26

27

28

In colder climates, English ivy (*left*) that you've grown outdoors all summer can be brought indoors and kept as a houseplant in winter.

An interesting houseplant display (*top right*); snake plant (*bottom right*), a striking and long-lived indoor plant

Houseplants generally only need fertilizer when they are actively growing. Always use a weak fertilizer to avoid burning the roots. Never feed plants when they are very dry. Moisten the soil by watering and then feed a couple of days later.

When repotting, go up by only one size at a time. In general the new pot should be no more than 2–4" (5–10 cm) larger in diameter than the previous pot. If you find your soil drying out too frequently, then you may wish to use a larger pot that will stay moist for longer.

Keep in mind that many common houseplants are tropical and dislike hot, dry conditions. Most houseplants will thrive in cooler, moister conditions than you will provide in your home. Always turn thermostats down at night and provide moist conditions by sitting pots on pebble trays. Water in the pebble tray can evaporate but won't soak excessively into the soil of the pot because the pebbles hold it above the water.

Here are a few easy-to-grow, toxin-absorbing houseplants:

- Bamboo Palm (*Camaedorea erumpens*)
- Chinese Evergreen (*Aglaonema modestum*)
- Dragon Tree (*Dracaena marginata*)
- English Ivy (*Hedera helix*)
- Gerbera Daisy (*Gerbera jamesonii*)
- Peace Lily (*Spathiphyllum* 'Mauna Loa')
- Pot Mum (*Chrysanthemum morifolium*)
- Snake Plant (*Sansevieria trifasciata*)
- Spider Plant (*Chlorophytum cosmosum*)
- Weeping Fig (*Ficus benjamina*)

DECEMBER

29

30

Most indoor plant pests can be controlled by wiping leaves with a damp sponge. More difficult pests can be controlled with insecticidal soap.

31

A bouquet of cheerful gerberas (*below & far right*) will brighten a drab winter day and remind you of summer, when these flowers were growing in your garden.

Cacti (*near right*) make good houseplants because they are undemanding and tolerate the dry air found in some homes quite well.

Coastal gardeners may not have problems providing sufficient humidity for houseplants, but they do need to provide more light, so keep plants near windows.

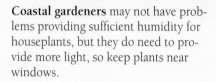

Dust on plants is more than just an eyesore. It prevents plants from making full use of the light they receive. Clean leaves regularly with a damp cloth or sponge, or place them in the shower and let the water stream wash away any dust.

Plants can be grouped together in large containers to more easily meet the needs of the plants. Cacti can be planted together in a gritty soil mix and placed in a dry, bright location. Moisture- and humidity-loving plants can be planted in a large terrarium where moisture levels remain higher.

There's nothing like treating yourself to a bouquet of fresh flowers (*above*) when you're feeling the doldrums of winter. Many beautiful varieties are available. Watch for some of the more exotic plants from South America and Australia at grocery stores and florist shops.

RESOURCES

BOOKS

Acorn, John and Ian Sheldon. 2001. *Bugs of Washington and Oregon.* Lone Pine Publishing, Edmonton, AB.

Beck, Alison and Marianne Binetti. 2000. *Perennials for Washington and Oregon.* Lone Pine Publishing, Edmonton, AB.

Beck, Alison and Marianne Binetti. 2000. *Annuals for Washington and Oregon.* Lone Pine Publishing, Edmonton, AB.

Beck, Alison and Marianne Binetti. 2001. *Tree and Shrub Gardening for Washington and Oregon.* Lone Pine Publishing, Edmonton, AB.

Brickell, C., T.J. Cole and J.D. Zuk, eds. 1996. *Reader's Digest A–Z Encyclopedia of Garden Plants.* The Reader's Digest Association Ltd., Montreal, PQ.

Bubel, Nancy. 1988. *The New Seed-Starters Handbook.* Rodale Press, Emmaus, PA.

Cavendish Gardens. 1999. *Handbook of Pruning and Training.* Cavendish Books, Vancouver, BC.

Courtier, Jane and Graham Clarke. 1997. *Indoor Plants: The Essential Guide to Choosing and Caring for Houseplants.* Reader's Digest, Westmount, PQ.

Ellis, B.W. and F.M. Bradley, eds. 1996. *The Organic Gardener's Handbook of Natural Insect and Disease Control.* Rodale Press, Emmaus, PA.

Feeney, Stephanie and Debra Prinzing. 2002. *The Northwest Gardeners' Resource Directory,* 9th Edition. Seattle, WA.

Francko, David A. 2003. *Palms Won't Grow Here and Other Myths: Warm-Climate Plants for Cooler Areas.* Timber Press, Portland, OR.

Heintzelman, Donald S. 2001. *The Complete Backyard Birdwatcher's Home Companion.* Ragged Mountain Press, Camden, ME.

Hill, Lewis. 1991. *Secrets of Plant Propagation.* Storey Communications Inc., Pownal, VT.

Jalbert, Brad and Laura Peters. 2003. *Roses for Washington and Oregon.* Lone Pine Publishing, Edmonton, AB.

Lyons, C.P. 1999. *Trees and Shrubs of Washington.* Lone Pine Publishing, Edmonton, AB.

McHoy, Peter. 2002. *Houseplants.* Hermes House, New York, NY.

McVicar, Jekka. 1997. *Jekka's Complete Herb Book.* Raincoast Books, Vancouver, BC.

Merilees, Bill. 1989. *Attracting Backyard Wildlife: A Guide for Nature Lovers.* Voyageur Press, Stillwater, MN.

Robinson, Peter. 1997. *Complete Guide to Water Gardening.* Reader's Digest, Westmount, PQ.

Thompson, Peter. 1992. *Creative Propagation: A Grower's Guide.* Timber Press, Portland, OR.

ONLINE RESOURCES

Attracting Wildlife to your garden.com. How to make your backyard inviting to compatible and beneficial creatures. www.attracting-wildlife-to-your-garden.com

Evergreen Foundation. A national environmental organization that provides tools to create healthy outdoor spaces. www.evergreen.ca/en/index.html

Green Is Life. Organic gardening information and links and a list of gardens, parks and greenspaces to visit throughout Oregon. www.greenislife.com

I Can Garden. Information and a gardening forum. www.icangarden.com/

I Love Gardens. An extensive list of gardens and arboretums to visit throughout Washington and Oregon. www.ilovegardens.com

Juniper and Sage. Organic gardening information for central Oregon gardeners. www.juniperandsage.com/

Northwest Gardening. Two Pacific Northwest landscape designers offer information on gardening in our region. www.nwgardening.com

Oregon State University. Master Gardener program. www.osu.orst.edu/extension/mg/

Organic Gardening. Information and a magazine for organic gardeners. www.organicgardening.com

Slugs and Salal. Everything you need to know about gardening in the Pacific Northwest. www.slugsandsalal.com

Soil Soup. Compost tea information. www.soilsoup.com

Specialty Nurseries Northwest. Marketplace includes a list of nurseries, garden shops, display gardens, garden shows and a forum for Northwest gardeners. www.specialtynurseries.com/

Terra Nova Nurseries. List of interesting and diverse perennials, most of which were bred by Terra Nova, based in Canby, Oregon. www.terranovanurseries.com

Territorial Seed Company. Online seed catalogue, including herbs, annuals, perennials, fruit, vegetables and supplies. Based in Cottage Grove, Oregon. www.territorialseed.com

Turf Resource Center and The Lawn Institute. The latest data regarding turfgrass. www.TurfGrassSod.org www.LawnInstitute.com

Two Rainyside Gardeners. Information about gardening in the Pacific Northwest. www.rainyside.com

University of Illinois Extension. Information on houseplant care, annuals, perennials, growing vegetables and fruit, diseases and insects, herbs and seasonal features. www.urbanext.uiuc.edu/houseplants/

University of Washington and the Center for Urban Horticulture. Extensive lists of resource material, including a digital library, collections and services links, resource center and a calendar of coming events.www.depts.washington.edu/hortlib /resources/hort_web_sites/arboreta.shtml

US Composting Council. www.compostingcouncil.org/links.cfm

Washington County Cooperative Recycling Program. Recycling and composting information for the Portland area. www.co.washington.or.us/deptmts/hhs/ws te_rcy/waste_l.htm

SOIL-TESTING FACILITIES
Washington:
AgriNorthwest
PO Box 2308
TriCities, WA 99302
509-783-0694

Cascade Analytical Inc.
3019 G.S. Center Road
Wenatchee, WA 98801
509-662-1888

Kuo Testing Labs Inc.
337 South 1 Avenue
Othello, WA 99344
509-488-0112
www.kuotesting.com
email: kuotest@atnet.net
Laucks Testing Laboratory
940 S. Harney Street

Laucks Testing Laboratory
940 S. Harney Street
Seattle, WA 98108
206-767-5060

Soil Search Labs
42125 S. Morton Road
Kennewick, WA 99337
509-585-8875
email: soilsrch@gte.net

SoilTest Farm Consultants
2925 Driggs Drive
Moses Lake, WA 98837
509-765-1622
www.soiltestlab.com

Oregon:
Analytical Laboratory & Consultants Inc.
361 West 5th Avenue
Eugene, OR 97401
541-485-8404 or 1-800-262-5973
email: anlabinc@rio.com

Neilson Research Corporation
245 South Grape Street
Medford, OR 97501
541-770-5678

North Creek Analytical
20332 Empire Avenue, F-1
Bend, OR 97701
541-383-9810

Pacific Agricultural Laboratory
12505 NW Cornell Road
Portland, OR 97229
503-626-7943
email: sthun@pacaglab.com

Waterlab Corp.
2603-12th Street SE
Salem, OR 97302-2154
503-363-0473

HORTICULTURAL SOCIETIES
Washington:
Northwest Horticultural Society
University of Washington
Box 354115
Seattle, WA 98195-4115
206-527-1794
www.northwesthort.org
email: nhsemail@compuserve.com

Washington State Federation of Garden
Clubs 425-822-7275
(Contact: Mary Ellen Kennedy)
www.washingtongardenclubs.org
email: info@WashingtonGardenClubs.org

Whatcom Horticultural Society
PO Box 4443
Bellingham, WA 98227
360-738-6833
www.home.earthlink.net/~cedarcroft/
WhatcomHS

Oregon:
Clatsop County Master Gardener Society
2001 Marine Drive, Room 210
Astoria, OR 97103
503-325-8573 (Contact: Justin Williams)
email: clatsopmg@hotmail.com

Oregon Horticultural Society
2015 Yamhill
McMinnville, OR 97128
503-472-7910

Oregon State Federation of Garden Clubs
represents over 300 garden clubs and
horticultural societies
541-354-1139
(Contact: Jeanne Marie Davis)
email: dmaccee@aol.com

**National Garden Clubs with state
affiliates:**
American Horticultural Society
7931 East Boulevard Drive
Alexandria, VA 22308
1-800-777-7931
www.ahs.org

National Garden Clubs
represents 50 state garden clubs, 8858
member garden clubs and 235,316
members
4401 Magnolia Avenue
St. Louis, MO 63110
314-776-7574
www.gardenclub.org
email: headquarters@gardenclub.org

GARDENS TO VISIT

Washington:

Bellevue Botanical Garden
12001 Main Street
Bellevue, WA 98005
425-452-2750
www.bellevuebotanical.org

Big Rock Garden Park
Sylvan Street and Illinois Lane
Bellingham, WA 98226
360-676-6985

Bloedel Reserve
(reservations required)
7571 NE Dolphin Drive
Bainbridge Island, WA 98110
206-842-7631
www.bloedelreserve.org

DeGoede Bulb Farms and Gardens
409 Mossyrock Road
Mossyrock, WA 98584
360-983-3773

Heronswood Nursery
(reservations required)
7530 NE 288 Street
Kingston, WA 98346
360-297-4172
www.heronswood.com/

The Centennial Rose Garden
330 Schmidt Place SW
Tumwater, WA 98501-3338
www.olyrose.org/public.htm

The Seattle Chinese Garden
South Seattle Community College
6000 16th Avenue SW
Seattle, WA
206-282-8040 ext.100
www.seattle-chinese-garden.org

Washington Park Arbotetum
University of Washington
2300 Aboretum Drive E
Seattle, WA 98112
206-325-4510 or 206-543-8800

Oregon:

Asahel Bush House,
Bush Pasture Park and Gardens
600 SE Mission Street
Salem, OR 97302
503-363-4714 or 503-581-2228

Berry Botanic Garden
11505 SW Summerville Avenue
Portland, OR 97219-8309
503-636-4112

International Rose Test Garden
Washington Park
400 SW Kingston Avenue
Portland, OR 97201
503-823-PLAY
www.parks.ci.portland.or.us
email: pkweb@ci.portland.or.us

Jackson and Perkins Test
and Display Gardens
2836 Pacific Highway
Medford, OR 97501
541-776-2277
www.jacksonandperkins.com/

Shore Acres State Park
and Botanical Gardens
10965 Cape Arago Highway
Coos Bay, OR 97420
541-888-3732 or 1-800-551-6949

Tallina's Wedding Gardens and
Conservatory
15791 SE Highway 224
Clackamas, OR 97015
503-658-6148

The Connie Hansen Garden
1931 NW 33rd Street
PO Box 776
Lincoln City, OR 97367
541-994-6338

The Garden of Awakening Orchids
(Lan Su Yuan, The Classical
Chinese Garden)
NW 3rd and Everett
Portland, OR 503-228-8131

WASHINGTON CLIMATE NORMALS
(Adapted from Western Regional Climate Center data as
posted on the Western Regional Climate Center website)

	CATEGORY	JAN	FEB	MAR	APR	MAY	JUN	JUL	AUG	SEP	OCT	NOV	DEC	YEAR
BELLINGHAM	DAILY MAXIMUM (°F)	43.1	47.7	51.1	56.4	62.4	66.8	71.3	71.4	67.1	58.4	49.6	44.5	57.5
	DAILY MINIMUM (°F)	31.3	34.0	35.9	40.0	45.3	50.5	53.2	53.2	48.2	42.1	36.7	33.1	42.0
	*PRECIPITATION (IN.)	4.62	3.53	2.97	2.68	2.12	1.75	1.24	1.37	1.85	3.49	5.07	4.85	35.55
	SNOWFALL (IN.)	5.1	1.7	1.8	0.1	0.0	0.0	0.0	0.0	0.0	0.1	0.9	4.0	13.7
OLYMPIA	DAILY MAXIMUM (°F)	44.3	49.1	53.3	59.1	65.8	71.0	77.0	77.0	71.6	60.6	50.4	44.8	60.3
	DAILY MINIMUM (°F)	31.4	32.7	33.7	36.5	41.5	46.6	49.4	49.4	45.2	39.5	35.5	32.7	39.5
	PRECIPITATION (IN.)	7.98	6.13	5.11	3.35	2.00	1.58	0.76	1.16	2.08	4.72	8.15	8.22	51.25
	SNOWFALL (IN.)	7.3	3.7	1.9	0.1	0.0	0.0	0.0	0.0	0.0	0.0	1.3	3.9	18.1
TRI-CITIES AREA	DAILY MAXIMUM (°F)	40.5	48.5	57.9	66.8	75.4	82.7	90.3	89.3	80.7	67.0	51.0	41.9	66.0
	DAILY MINIMUM (°F)	25.8	30.5	35.0	41.0	48.2	54.8	59.4	58.7	50.6	40.8	33.8	28.4	42.3
	PRECIPITATION (IN.)	1.02	0.72	0.63	0.48	0.56	0.49	0.22	0.25	0.27	0.53	0.97	1.01	7.16
	SNOWFALL (IN.)	3.2	1.8	0.3	0.0	0.0	0.0	0.0	0.0	0.0	0.0	0.7	2.6	8.7
SEATTLE	DAILY MAXIMUM (°F)	44.6	49.0	52.2	57.5	64.1	69.4	75.0	74.7	69.4	59.4	50.4	45.4	59.3
	DAILY MINIMUM (°F)	34.7	36.7	38.0	41.2	46.4	51.3	54.5	54.8	51.3	45.3	39.5	35.8	44.1
	PRECIPITATION (IN.)	5.70	4.21	3.75	2.51	1.69	1.44	0.78	1.09	1.78	3.47	6.00	5.85	38.27
	SNOWFALL (IN.)	5.1	1.7	1.3	0.1	0.0	0.0	0.0	0.0	0.0	0.0	0.8	2.6	11.7
SPOKANE	DAILY MAXIMUM (°F)	32.9	39.1	48.2	58.3	67.0	74.3	83.9	82.7	72.4	59.2	42.9	34.7	58.0
	DAILY MINIMUM (°F)	21.5	25.2	30.5	36.5	43.7	50.1	55.7	54.5	46.5	37.6	30.0	24.3	38.0
	PRECIPITATION (IN.)	1.99	1.57	1.38	1.11	1.39	1.21	0.56	0.62	0.81	1.18	2.10	2.19	16.11
	SNOWFALL (IN.)	13.0	7.7	3.4	0.5	0.1	0.0	0.0	0.0	0.0	0.3	5.4	11.2	41.8
WALLA WALLA	DAILY MAXIMUM (°F)	39.5	46.2	54.6	62.8	71.1	79.8	89.3	87.5	78.1	64.6	48.8	40.9	63.6
	DAILY MINIMUM (°F)	27.6	32.3	36.3	41.3	47.7	54.3	60.5	60.4	52.5	43.4	35.0	29.6	43.4
	PRECIPITATION (IN.)	2.32	1.73	1.95	1.66	1.78	1.20	0.60	0.77	0.88	1.69	2.54	2.33	19.45
	SNOWFALL (IN.)	6.4	3.0	1.2	0.0	0.0	0.0	0.0	0.0	0.0	0.1	1.9	5.1	17.7

* equivalent to rainfall

OREGON CLIMATE NORMALS
(Adapted from Western Regional Climate Center data as
posted on the Western Regional Climate Center website)

CATEGORY	JAN	FEB	MAR	APR	MAY	JUN	JUL	AUG	SEP	OCT	NOV	DEC	YEAR	
DAILY MAXIMUM (°F)	40.6	45.3	50.9	58.1	65.5	72.7	81.9	81	73.7	63	49.2	42	60.3	BEND
DAILY MINIMUM (°F)	21.3	24.1	26.4	29.7	35.3	40.8	45.3	44.4	38.2	32	27.1	23.3	32.3	
PRECIPITATION (IN.)	1.82	1.06	0.84	0.65	0.97	0.97	0.49	0.5	0.42	0.74	1.43	1.84	11.8	
SNOWFALL (IN.)	11.2	5.5	3.4	1.3	0.2	0.0	0.0	0.0	0.0	0.2	3.6	7.6	33.1	
DAILY MAXIMUM (°F)	46.2	51.3	55.7	61.0	67.4	73.8	82.1	81.8	76.6	64.4	52.7	46.8	63.3	EUGENE
DAILY MINIMUM (°F)	33.3	35.4	36.9	39.4	43.6	48.1	51.3	51.3	47.5	41.9	37.9	34.7	41.8	
PRECIPITATION (IN.)	7.54	5.59	5.10	2.96	2.36	1.38	0.44	0.78	1.43	3.69	7.44	7.79	46.49	
SNOWFALL (IN.)	3.3	0.9	0.5	0.0	0.0	0.0	0.0	0.0	0.0	0.0	0.2	1.1	6.0	
DAILY MAXIMUM (°F)	38.1	43.4	51.3	58.6	67.6	76.0	85.7	86.2	76.4	62.8	46.5	38.6	60.9	LA GRANDE
DAILY MINIMUM (°F)	24.0	27.0	30.7	35.0	41.8	48.4	52.9	51.8	43.7	35.4	30.4	24.6	37.1	
PRECIPITATION (IN.)	1.87	1.39	1.46	1.55	1.81	1.54	0.70	0.83	0.87	1.29	2.08	1.88	17.26	
SNOWFALL (IN.)	7.7	3.7	1.5	0.5	0.0	0.0	0.0	0.0	0.0	0.2	2.3	6.4	22.4	
DAILY MAXIMUM (°F)	45.7	53.1	58.4	64.9	72.8	80.6	89.9	89.4	83.0	69.2	53.3	45.1	67.1	MEDFORD
DAILY MINIMUM (°F)	30.4	32.5	35.1	38.4	43.8	49.9	54.9	54.0	47.7	40.1	34.5	31.5	41.1	
PRECIPITATION (IN.)	2.92	2.09	1.76	1.19	1.23	0.83	0.26	0.35	0.67	1.63	2.81	3.31	19.04	
SNOWFALL (IN.)	3.1	1.1	0.7	0.2	0.0	0.0	0.0	0.0	0.0	0.0	0.4	1.4	6.9	
DAILY MAXIMUM (°F)	44.9	50.4	55.3	60.8	67.3	73.0	79.6	79.7	74.8	63.7	52.4	46.1	62.3	PORTLAND
DAILY MINIMUM (°F)	33.6	35.9	38.2	41.7	47.3	52.7	56.5	56.7	51.8	45.0	39.4	35.4	44.5	
PRECIPITATION (IN.)	5.47	4.05	3.69	2.48	2.20	1.59	0.59	0.92	1.59	3.12	5.60	5.87	37.16	
SNOWFALL (IN.)	3.2	1.2	0.4	0.0	0.0	0.0	0.0	0.0	0.0	0.0	0.4	1.4	6.6	
DAILY MAXIMUM (°F)	45.9	50.9	55.8	61.4	68.1	74.2	82.0	81.9	76.6	64.6	52.7	47.0	63.4	SALEM
DAILY MINIMUM (°F)	32.7	34.4	36.3	38.9	43.5	48.3	51.1	51.1	47.3	42.0	37.4	34.4	41.4	
PRECIPITATION (IN.)	6.26	4.95	4.37	2.59	2.04	1.39	0.43	0.56	1.41	3.38	5.96	7.03	40.35	
SNOWFALL (IN.)	3.2	1.5	0.5	0.0	0.0	0.0	0.0	0.0	0.0	0.1	0.2	1.4	6.9	

WASHINGTON/OREGON CLIMATE EXTREMES
(Adapted from Western Regional Climate Center data as posted
on the Western Regional Climate Center website)

BELLINGHAM

Maximum (°F)	94 on August 9, 1960
Minimum (°F)	-2 on January 25, 1950
Daily Rainfall	3.3" on January 12, 1976
Snowfall (month)	34.5" in March, 1951

OLYMPIA

Maximum (°F)	104 on August 9, 1981
Minimum (°F)	-8 on January 1, 1979
Daily Rainfall	4.33" on November 19, 1962
Snowfall (month)	58.7" in January, 1969

TRI-CITIES AREA

Maximum (°F)	113 on August 5, 1961
Minimum (°F)	-22 on February 2, 1950
Daily Rainfall	1.12" on August 30, 1977
Snowfall (month)	20.5" in January, 1969

SEATTLE

Maximum (°F)	100 on July 20, 1994
Minimum (°F)	0.0 on January 31, 1950
Daily Rainfall	3.41" on November 20, 1959
Snowfall (month)	57.2" in January, 1950

SPOKANE

Maximum (°F)	108 on July 26, 1928
Minimum (°F)	-25 on December 30, 1968
Daily Rainfall	1.66" on June 17, 1897
Snowfall (month)	56.9" in January, 1950

WALLA WALLA

Maximum (°F)	114 on August 4, 1961
Minimum (°F)	-24 on December 30, 1968
Daily Rainfall	3.64" on July 23, 1992
Snowfall (month)	29.3" in January, 1969

BEND

Maximum (°F)	104 on July 25, 1928
Minimum (°F)	-26 on February 9, 1933
Daily Rainfall	2.72" on October 29, 1950
Snowfall (month)	56.5" in January, 1950

EUGENE

Maximum (°F)	108 on August 9, 1981
Minimum (°F)	-12 on December 8, 1972
Daily Rainfall	4.89" on December 5, 1981
Snowfall (month)	47.1" in January, 1969

LA GRANDE

Maximum (°F)	104 on August 4, 1978
Minimum (°F)	-18 on December 23, 1983
Daily Rainfall	2.7" on November 26, 1999
Snowfall (month)	29.5" in December, 1971

MEDFORD

Maximum (°F)	115 on July 20, 1946
Minimum (°F)	-6 on December 8, 1972
Daily Rainfall	3.3" on December 2, 1962
Snowfall (month)	22.6" in January, 1930

PORTLAND

Maximum (°F)	107 on July 30, 1965
Minimum (°F)	-3 on February 2, 1950
Daily Rainfall	2.69" on November 19, 1996
Snowfall (month)	41.4" in January, 1950

SALEM

Maximum (°F)	108 on July 15, 1941
Minimum (°F)	-12 on December 8, 1972
Daily Rainfall	4.3" on December 6, 1933
Snowfall (month)	30.8" in December, 1950